FANTE BUKOWSKI

Noah Van Sciver

FANTAGRAPHICS BOOKS

Editor and associate publisher: Eric Reynolds
Book design: Keeli McCarthy
Production: Paul Baresh
Publisher: Gary Groth

Fantagraphics Books, Inc.
Seattle, Washington, USA

Library of Congress Control Number: 2015935147
ISBN 978-1-60699-851-9

Second printing: June, 2016
Printed in China

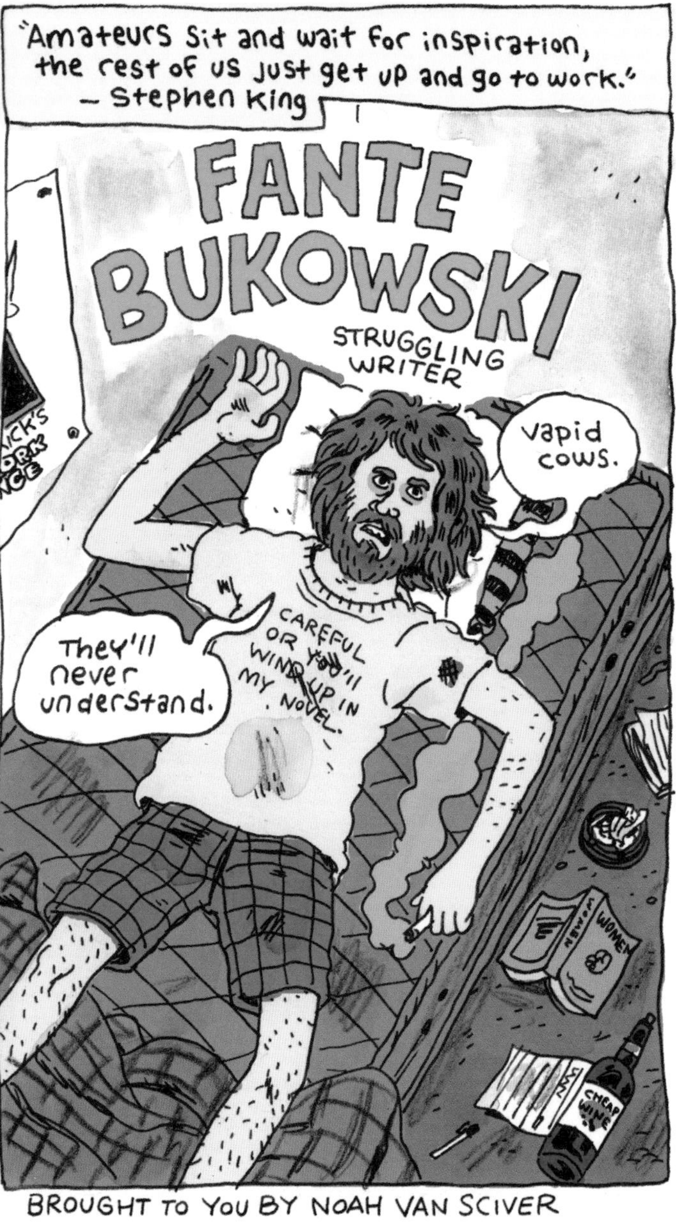
"Amateurs sit and wait for inspiration, the rest of us just get up and go to work." – Stephen King
FANTE BUKOWSKI
STRUGGLING WRITER
vapid cows.
They'll never understand.
CAREFUL OR YOU'LL WIND UP IN MY NOVEL.
WOMEN
WOMEN
CHEAP WINE

BROUGHT TO YOU BY NOAH VAN SCIVER

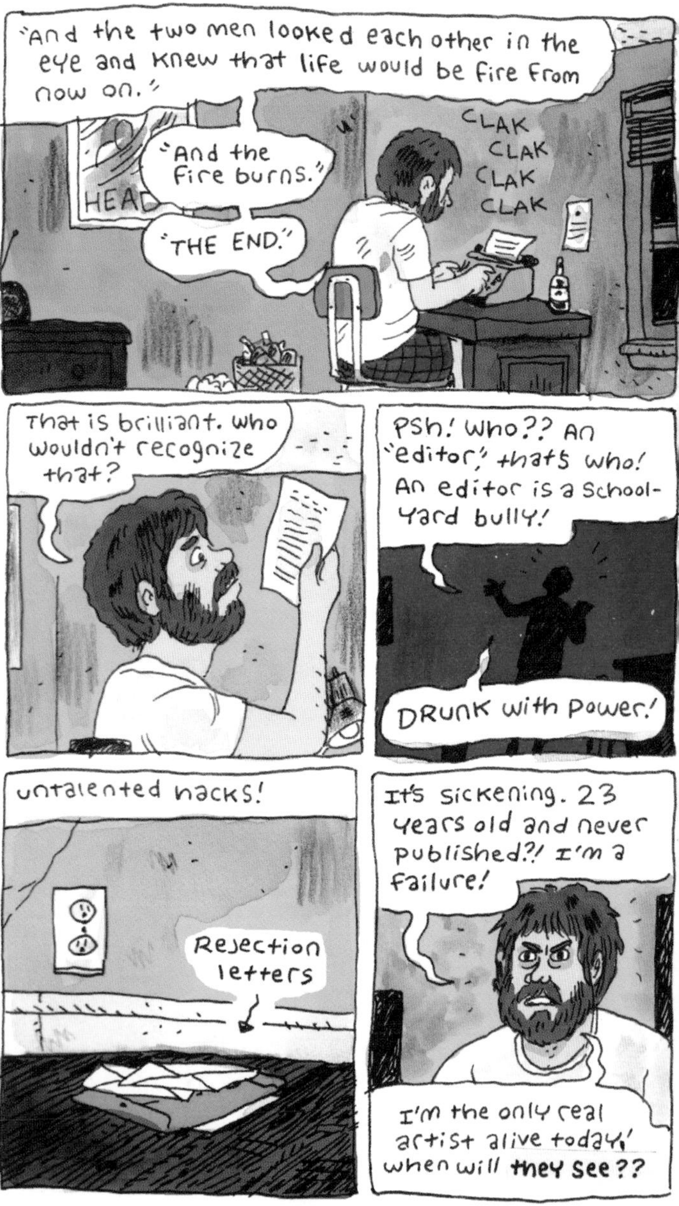
"And the two men looked each other in the eye and knew that life would be fire from now on."
HEAD
"And the fire burns."
"THE END."
CLAK
CLAK
CLAK
CLAK
That is brilliant. Who wouldn't recognize that?
Psh! Who?? An "editor," that's who! An editor is a school-yard bully!
DRUNK with power!
untalented hacks!
Rejection letters
It's sickening. 23 years old and never published?! I'm a failure!
I'm the only real artist alive today, when will they see??

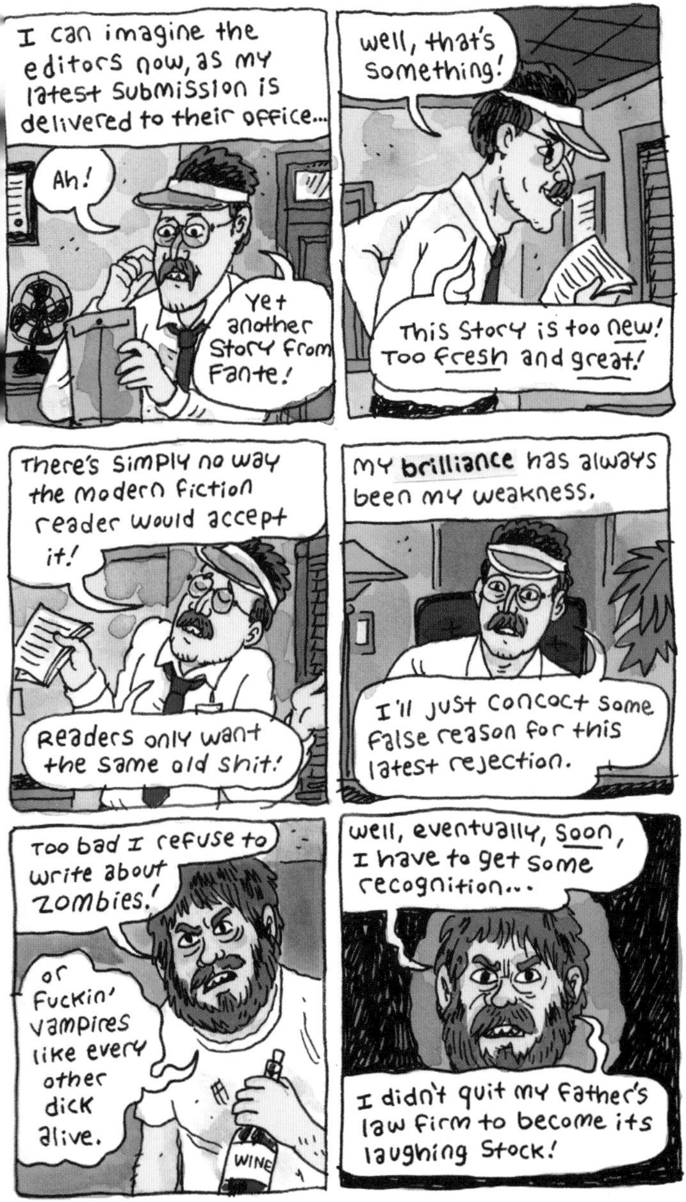
I can imagine the editors now, as my latest submission is delivered to their office...
Ah!
Yet another story from Fante!
Well, that's something!
This story is too new! Too fresh and great!
There's simply no way the modern fiction reader would accept it!
Readers only want the same old shit!
My brilliance has always been my weakness.
I'll just concoct some false reason for this latest rejection.
Too bad I refuse to write about zombies!
or fuckin' vampires like every other dick alive.
WINE
Well, eventually, soon, I have to get some recognition...
I didn't quit my father's law firm to become its laughing stock!

FANTE BUKOWSKI STAYS UP

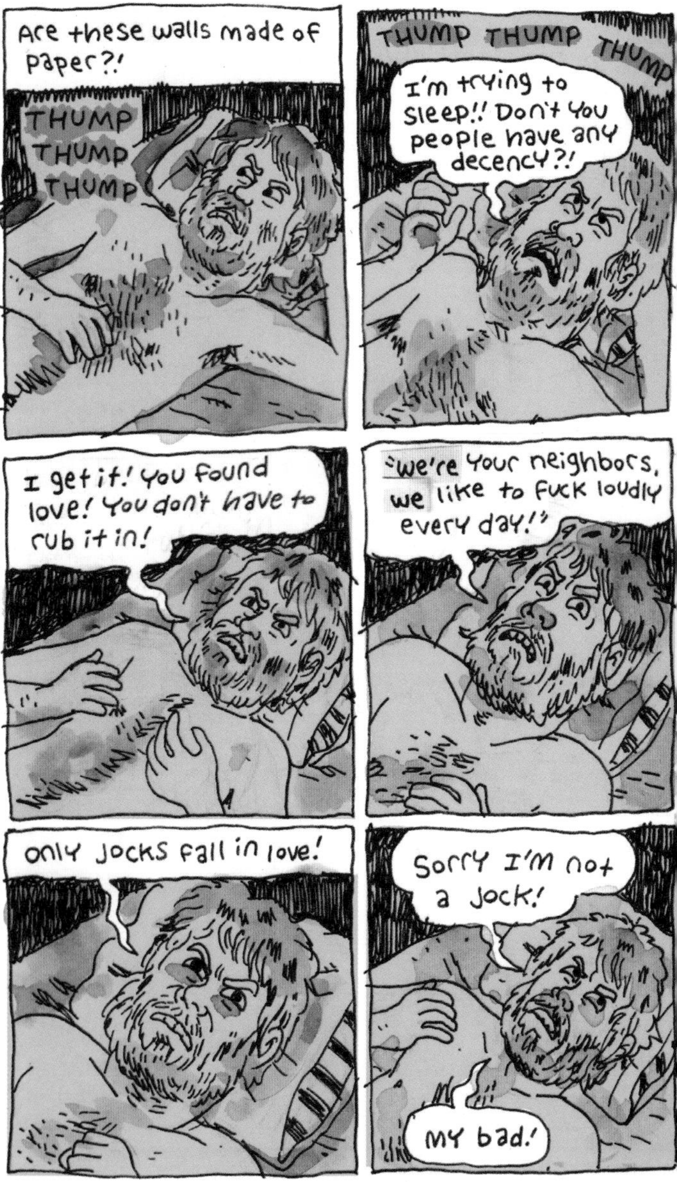
Are these walls made of paper?!
THUMP THUMP THUMP
THUMP THUMP THUMP
I'm trying to sleep!! Don't you people have any decency?!
I get it! You found love! You don't have to rub it in!
"We're your neighbors, we like to fuck loudly every day!"
Only jocks fall in love!
Sorry I'm not a jock!
My bad!

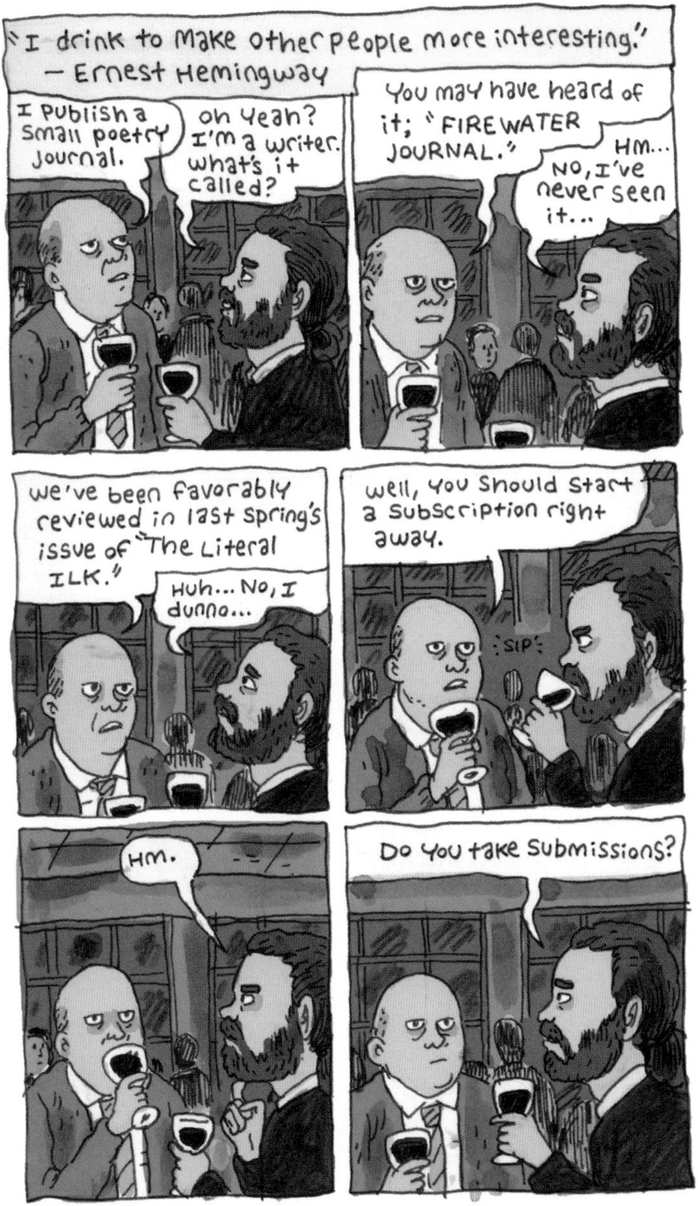
"I drink to make other people more interesting."
— Ernest Hemingway
I publish a small poetry journal.
Oh yeah? I'm a writer. what's it called?
You may have heard of it; "FIREWATER JOURNAL."
Hm... No, I've never seen it...
we've been favorably reviewed in last spring's issue of "The Literal ILK."
Huh... No, I dunno...
well, you should start a subscription right away.
SIP
HM.
Do you take submissions?

who is that guy over in the corner? He seems popular.

That's Ralph Bigsburgh. A highly-respected agent.

He discovered R.L. STINE.

Oh Yeah? ...I should go say "hello."

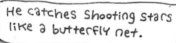

He catches Shooting stars like a butterfly net.

And he's queer like the dickens.

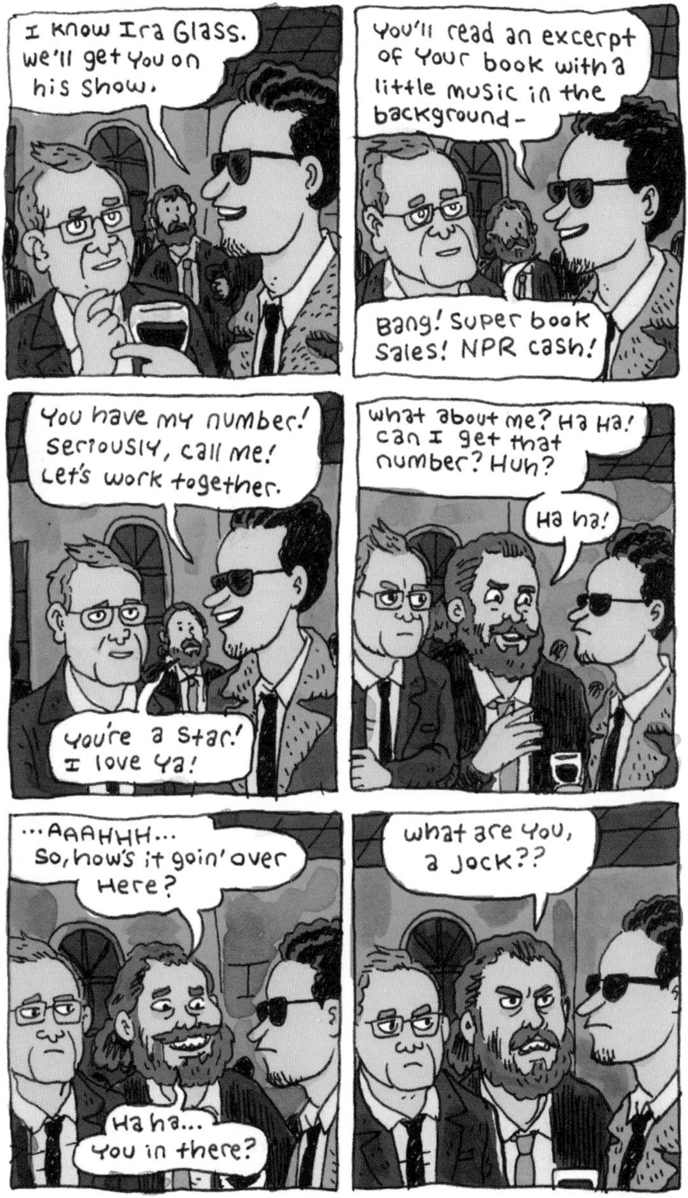
I know Ira Glass. we'll get you on his show.
You'll read an excerpt of your book with a little music in the background-
Bang! Super book sales! NPR cash!
You have my number! seriously, call me! Let's work together.
You're a star! I love ya!
what about me? Ha Ha! can I get that number? Huh?
Ha ha!
...AAAHHH... So, how's it goin' over Here?
Ha ha... You in there?
what are you, a Jock??

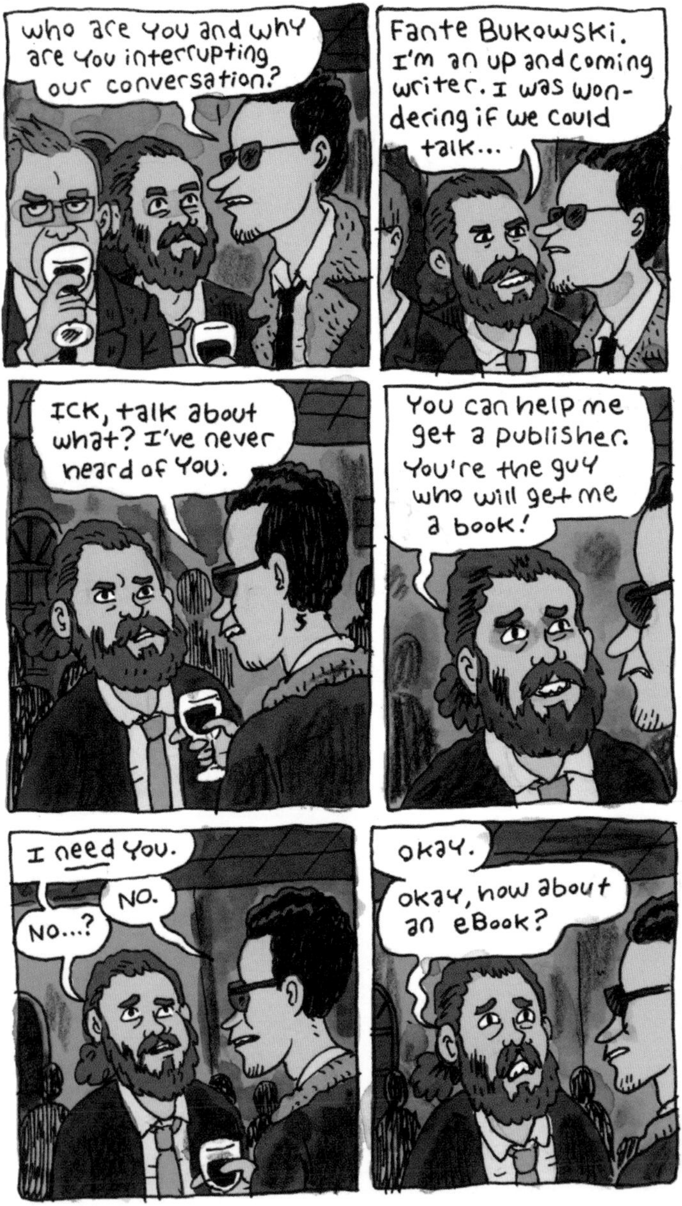
who are you and why are you interrupting our conversation?
Fante Bukowski. I'm an up and coming writer. I was wondering if we could talk...
ICK, talk about what? I've never heard of you.
You can help me get a publisher. You're the guy who will get me a book!
I need you.
NO.
NO...?
okay.
okay, how about an eBook?

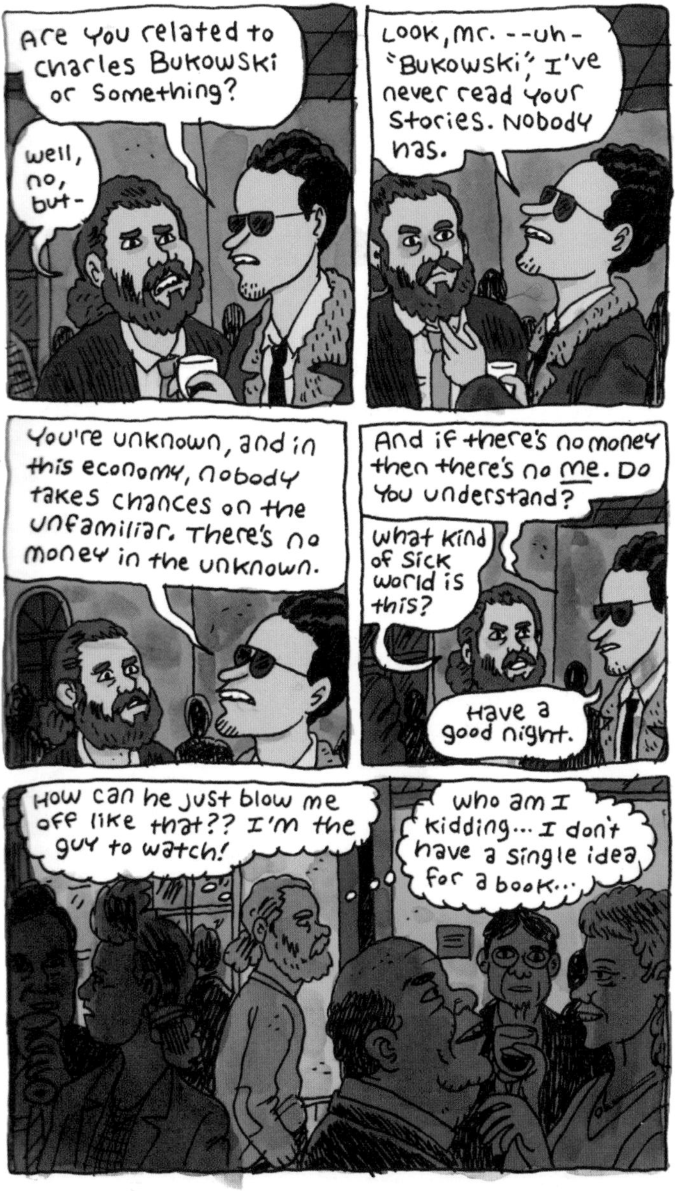
Are you related to Charles Bukowski or something?
well, no, but-
Look, Mr. --uh- "Bukowski," I've never read your stories. Nobody has.
You're unknown, and in this economy, nobody takes chances on the unfamiliar. There's no money in the unknown.
And if there's no money then there's no me. Do you understand?
what kind of sick world is this?
Have a good night.
How can he just blow me off like that?? I'm the guy to watch!
who am I kidding... I don't have a single idea for a book...

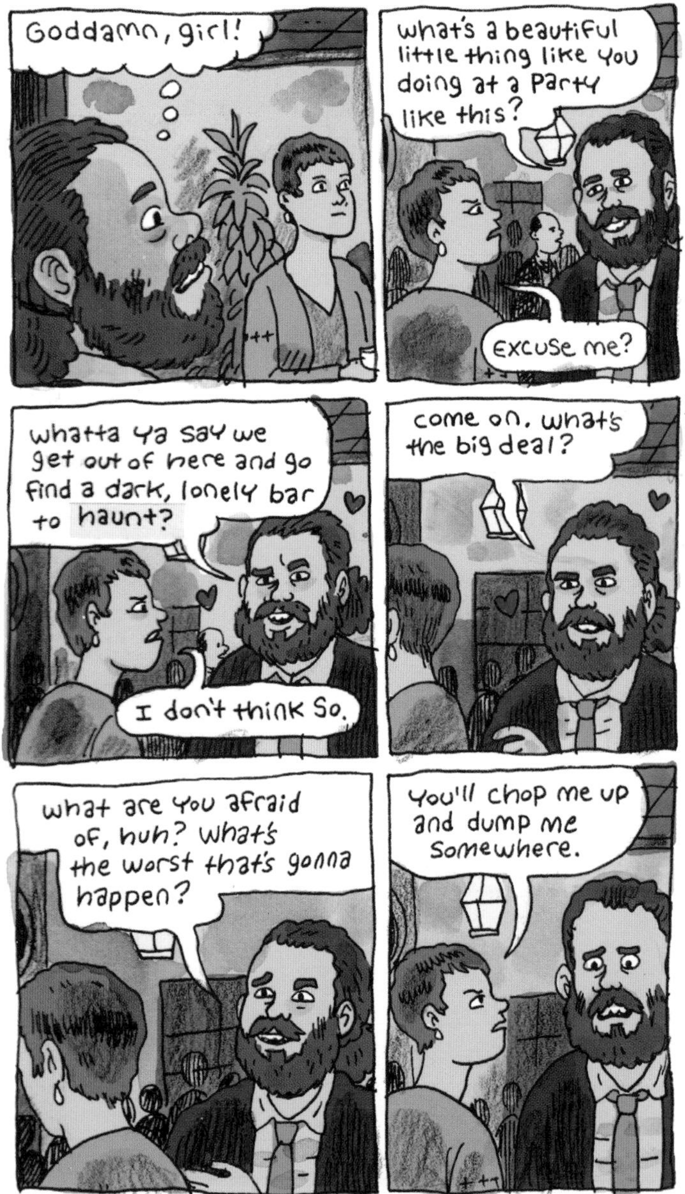
Goddamn, girl!
what's a beautiful little thing like you doing at a party like this?
Excuse me?
whatta ya say we get out of here and go find a dark, lonely bar to haunt?
I don't think so.
come on. what's the big deal?
what are you afraid of, huh? what's the worst that's gonna happen?
You'll chop me up and dump me somewhere.

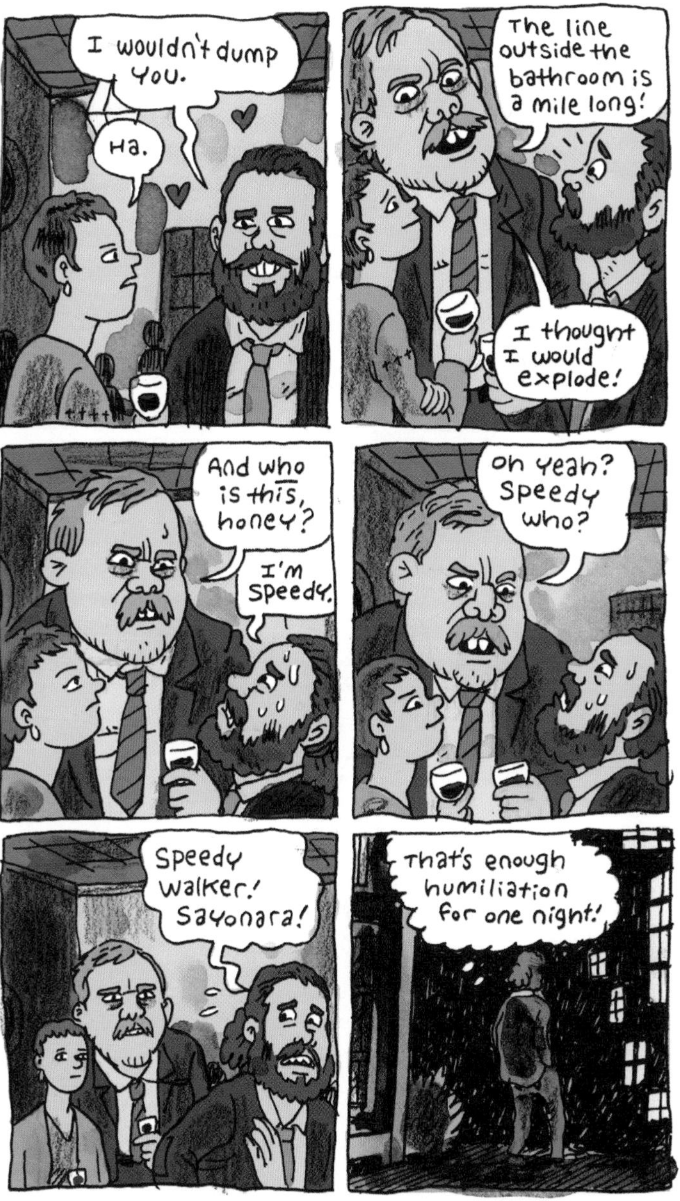
I wouldn't dump you.
Ha.
The line outside the bathroom is a mile long!
I thought I would explode!
And who is this, honey?
I'm speedy.
oh yeah? Speedy who?
Speedy walker! Sayonara!
That's enough humiliation for one night!

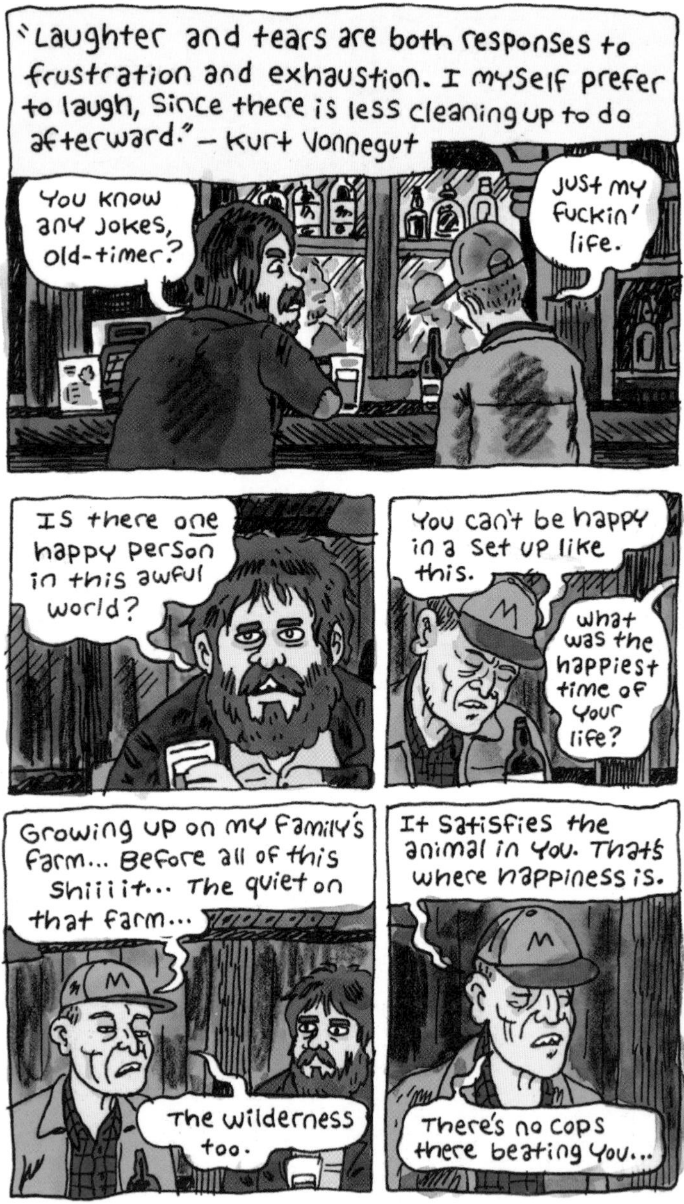
"Laughter and tears are both responses to frustration and exhaustion. I myself prefer to laugh, since there is less cleaning up to do afterward." — Kurt Vonnegut
You know any jokes, old-timer?
Just my fuckin' life.
Is there one happy person in this awful world?
You can't be happy in a set up like this.
What was the happiest time of your life?
Growing up on my family's farm... Before all of this shiiiit... The quiet on that farm...
The wilderness too.
It satisfies the animal in you. That's where happiness is.
There's no cops there beating you...

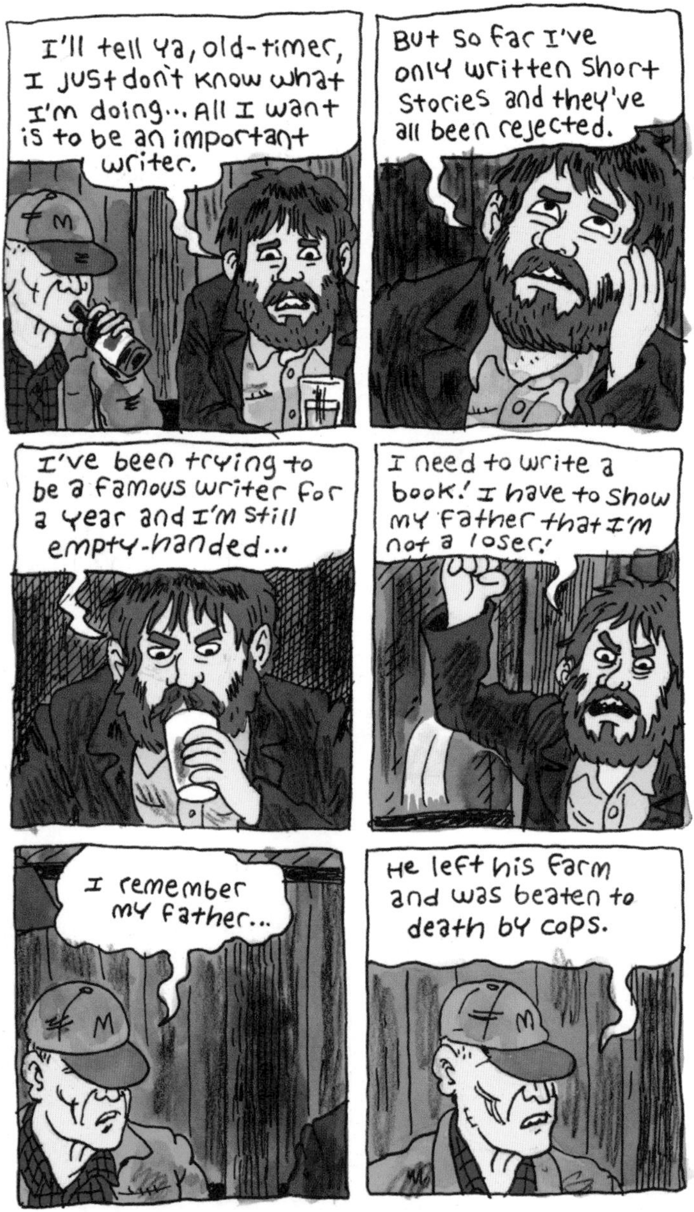
I'll tell ya, old-timer, I just don't know what I'm doing... All I want is to be an important writer.
But so far I've only written short stories and they've all been rejected.
I've been trying to be a famous writer for a year and I'm still empty-handed...
I need to write a book! I have to show my father that I'm not a loser!
I remember my father...
He left his farm and was beaten to death by cops.

FANTE WALKS HOME

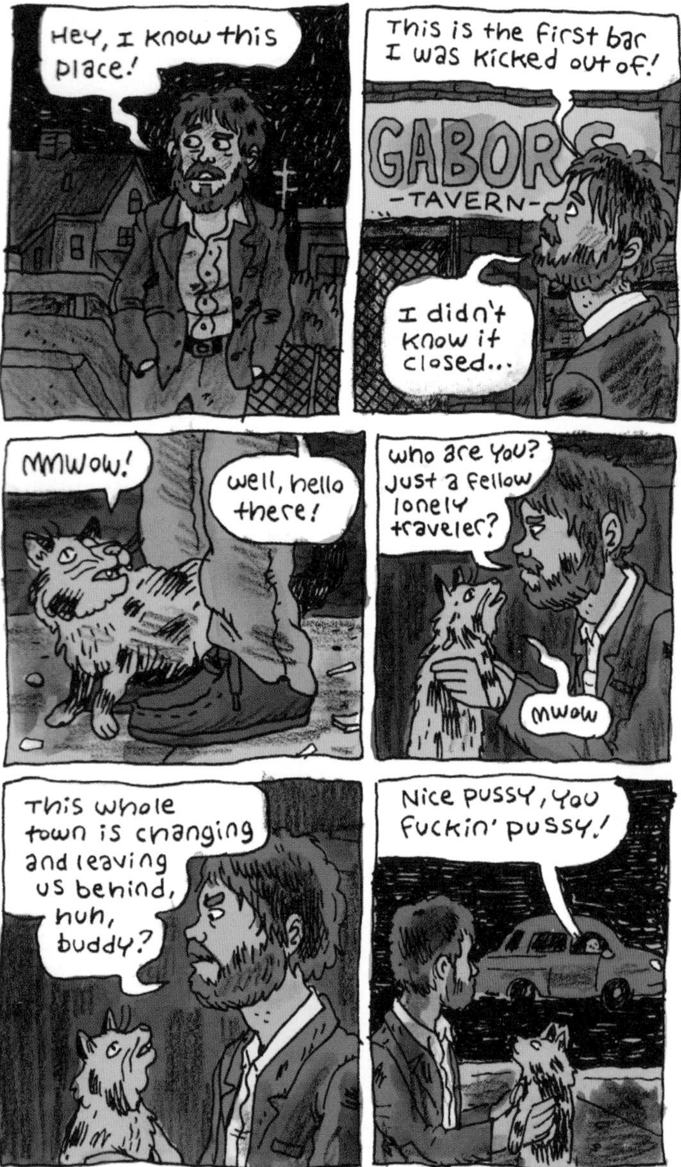

Hey, I know this place!
This is the first bar I was kicked out of!
GABOR'S
-TAVERN-
I didn't know it closed...
MMWOW!
well, hello there!
who are you? Just a fellow lonely traveler?
MWOW
This whole town is changing and leaving us behind, huh, buddy?
Nice pussy, you fuckin' pussy!

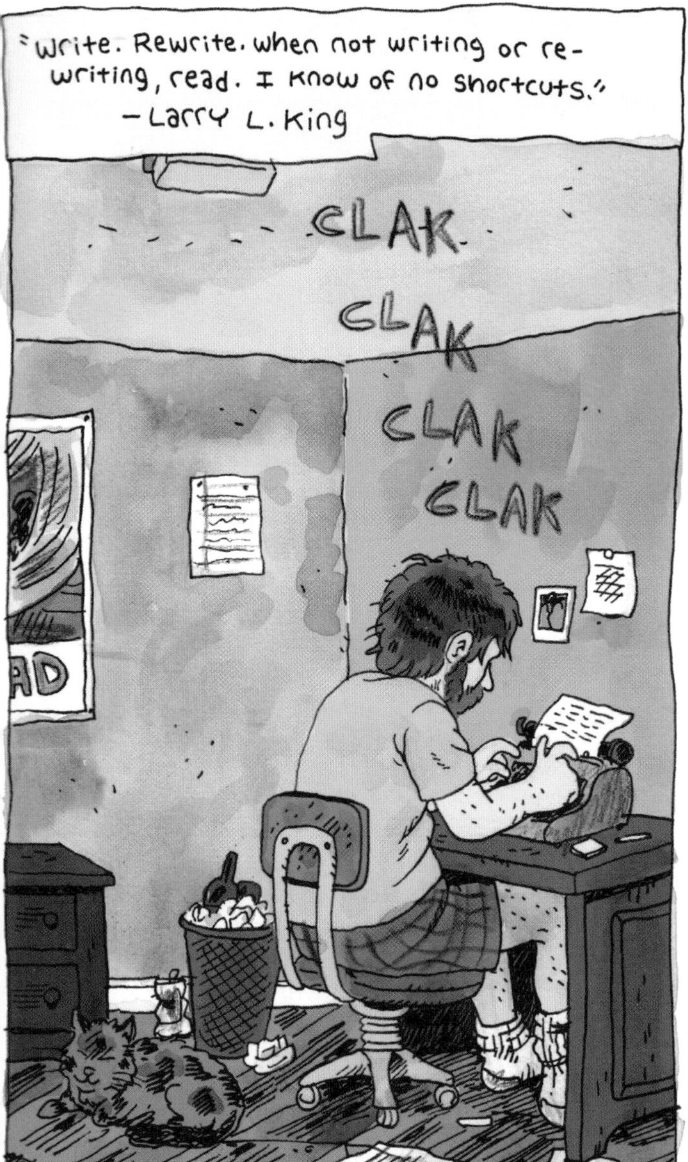
"Write. Rewrite. When not writing or re-writing, read. I know of no shortcuts."
—Larry L. King
CLAK
CLAK
CLAK
CLAK
AD

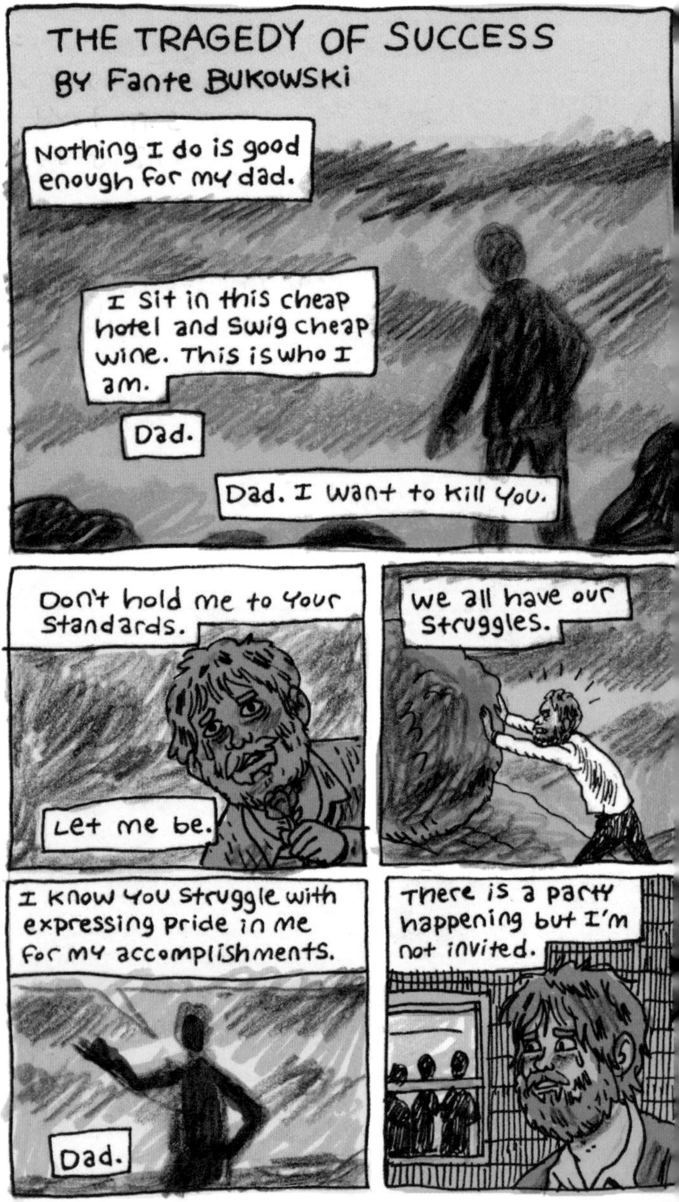

THE TRAGEDY OF SUCCESS
BY Fante BUKOWSKi
Nothing I do is good enough for my dad.
I sit in this cheap hotel and swig cheap wine. This is who I am.
Dad.
Dad. I want to kill you.
Don't hold me to your standards.
Let me be.
We all have our struggles.
I know you struggle with expressing pride in me for my accomplishments.
Dad.
There is a party happening but I'm not invited.

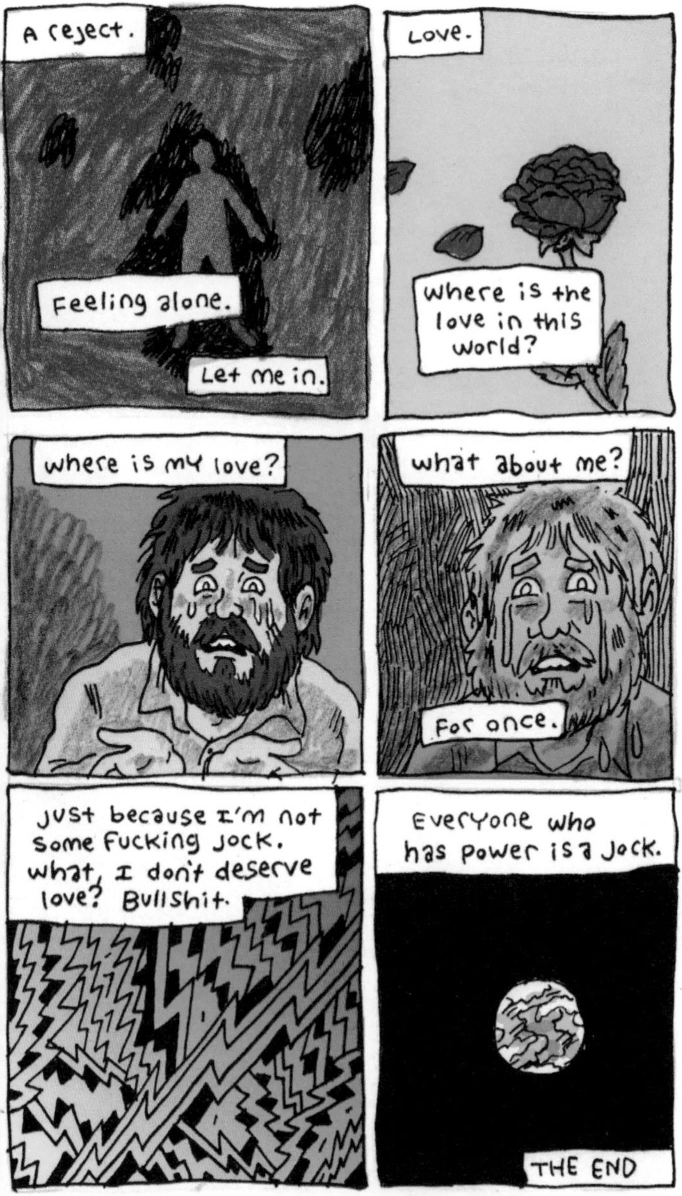
A reject.
Feeling alone.
Let me in.
Love.
Where is the love in this world?
Where is my love?
What about me?
For once.
Just because I'm not some fucking jock. What, I don't deserve love? Bullshit.
Everyone who has power is a jock.
THE END

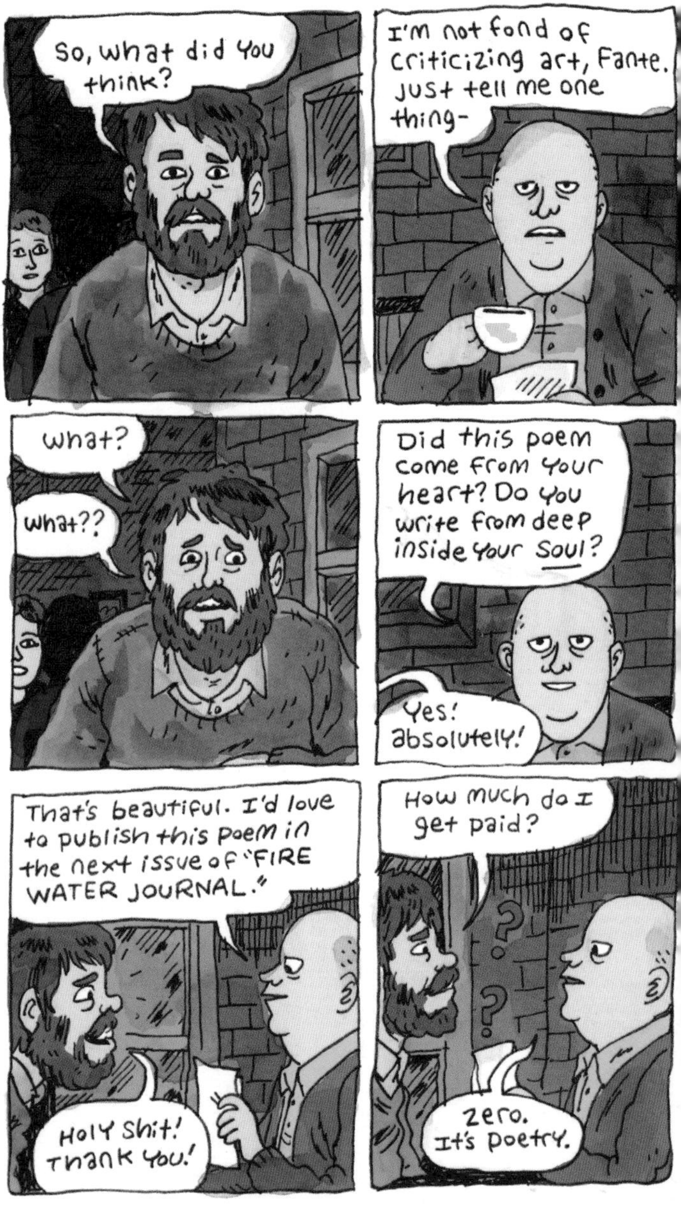
So, what did you think?
I'm not fond of criticizing art, Fante. Just tell me one thing-
what?
what??
Did this poem come from your heart? Do you write from deep inside your Soul?
Yes! absolutely!
That's beautiful. I'd love to publish this poem in the next issue of "FIRE WATER JOURNAL."
Holy Shit! Thank You!
How much do I get paid?
?
?
Zero. It's poetry.

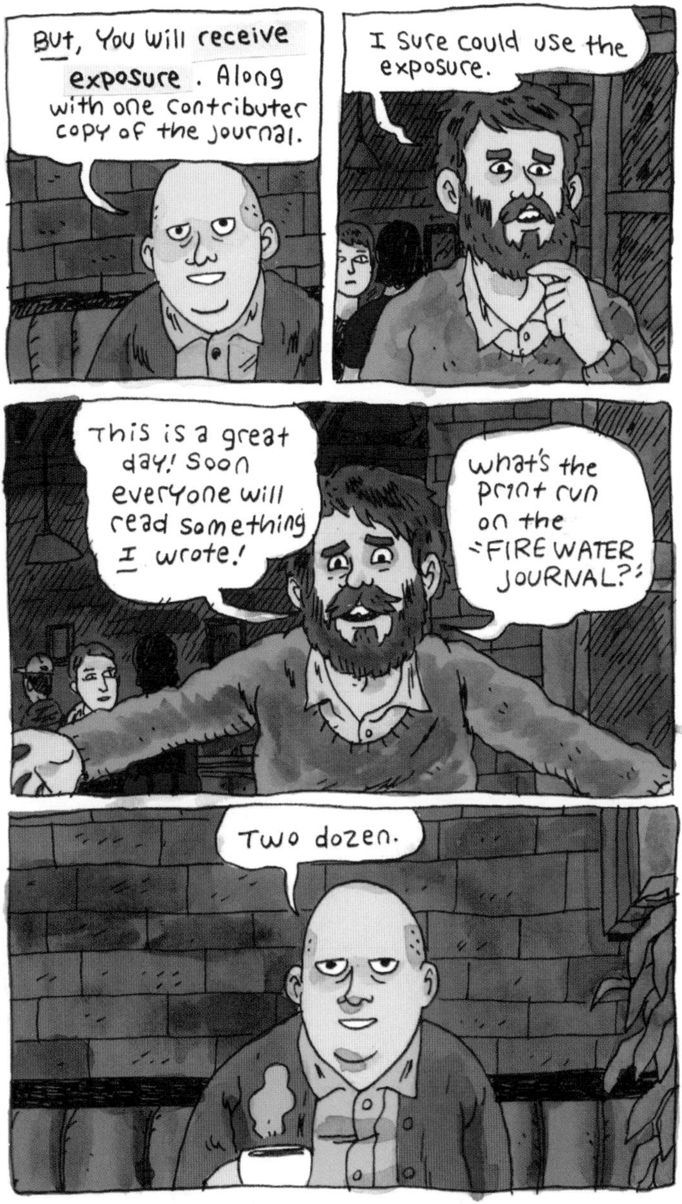
BUT, YOU WILL RECEIVE EXPOSURE. ALONG WITH ONE CONTRIBUTER COPY OF THE JOURNAL.
I SURE COULD USE THE EXPOSURE.
THIS IS A GREAT DAY! SOON EVERYONE WILL READ SOMETHING I WROTE!
WHAT'S THE PRINT RUN ON THE FIRE WATER JOURNAL?
TWO DOZEN.

FANTE NEEDS MONEY

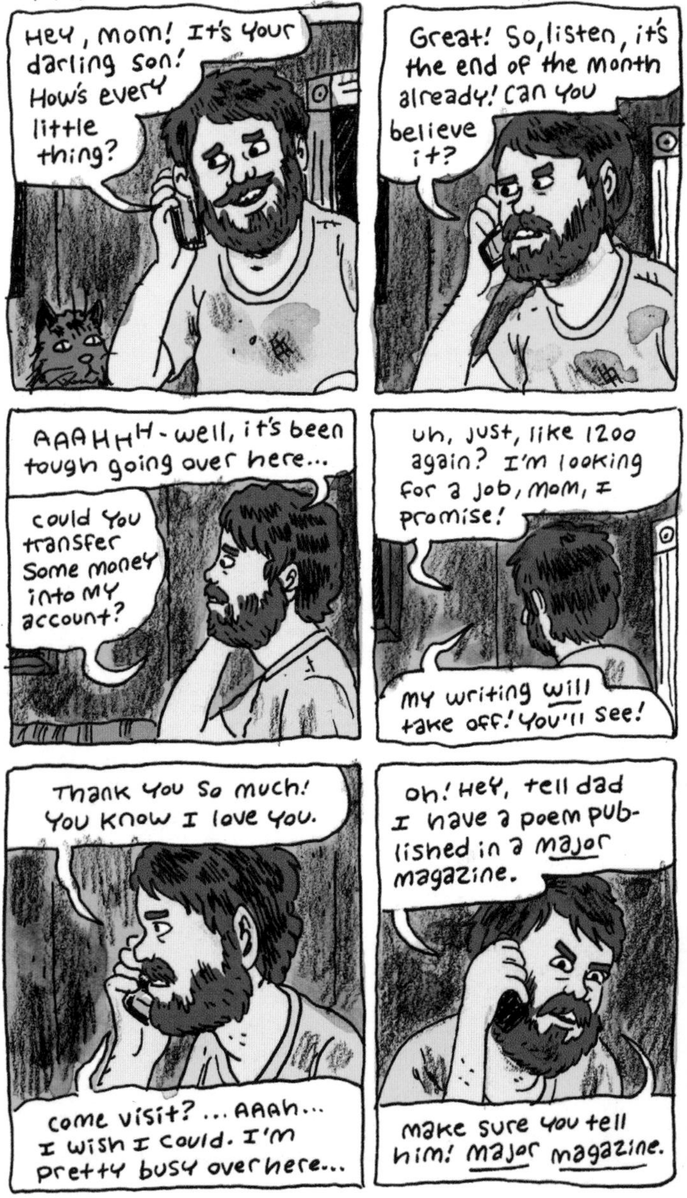
Hey, mom! It's your darling son! How's every little thing?
Great! So, listen, it's the end of the month already! Can you believe it?
AAAHHH - well, it's been tough going over here...
could you transfer some money into my account?
uh, just, like 1200 again? I'm looking for a job, mom, I promise!
my writing will take off! You'll see!
Thank you so much! You know I love you.
come visit? ... AAAh... I wish I could. I'm pretty busy over here...
oh! Hey, tell dad I have a poem pub-lished in a major magazine.
make sure you tell him! major magazine.

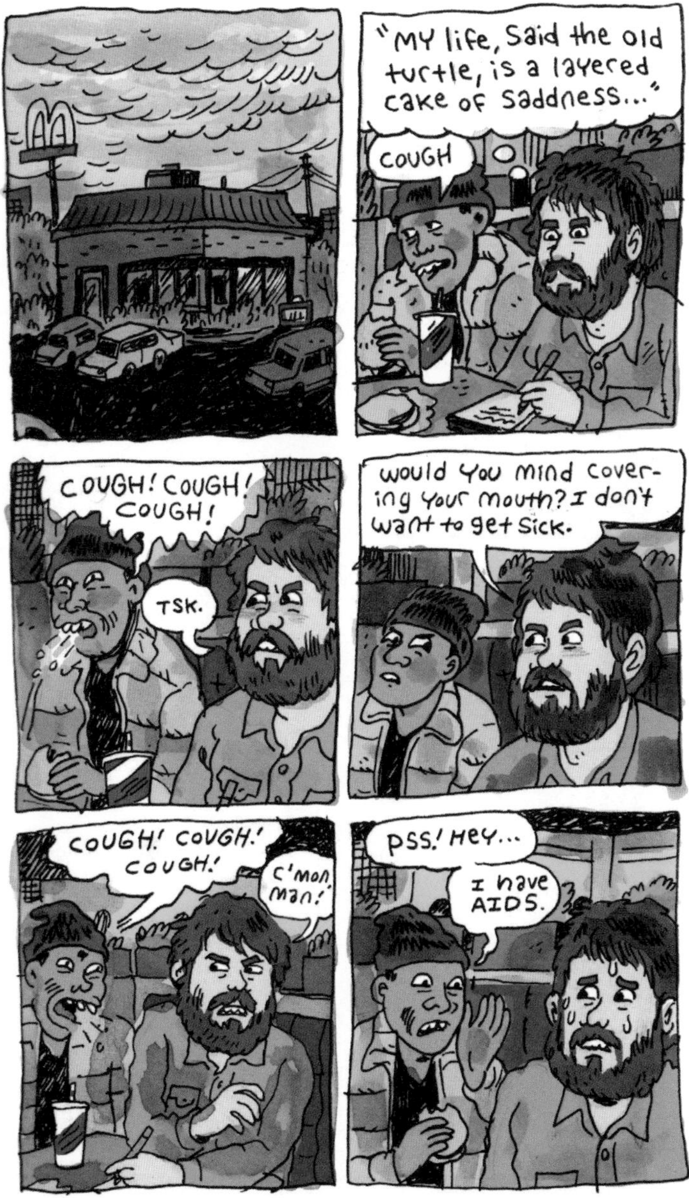
"MY life, Said the old turtle, is a layered cake of Saddness..."
COUGH
COUGH! COUGH! COUGH!
TSK.
would you mind covering your mouth? I don't want to get sick.
COUGH! COUGH! COUGH!
C'mon man!
PSS! Hey...
I have AIDS.

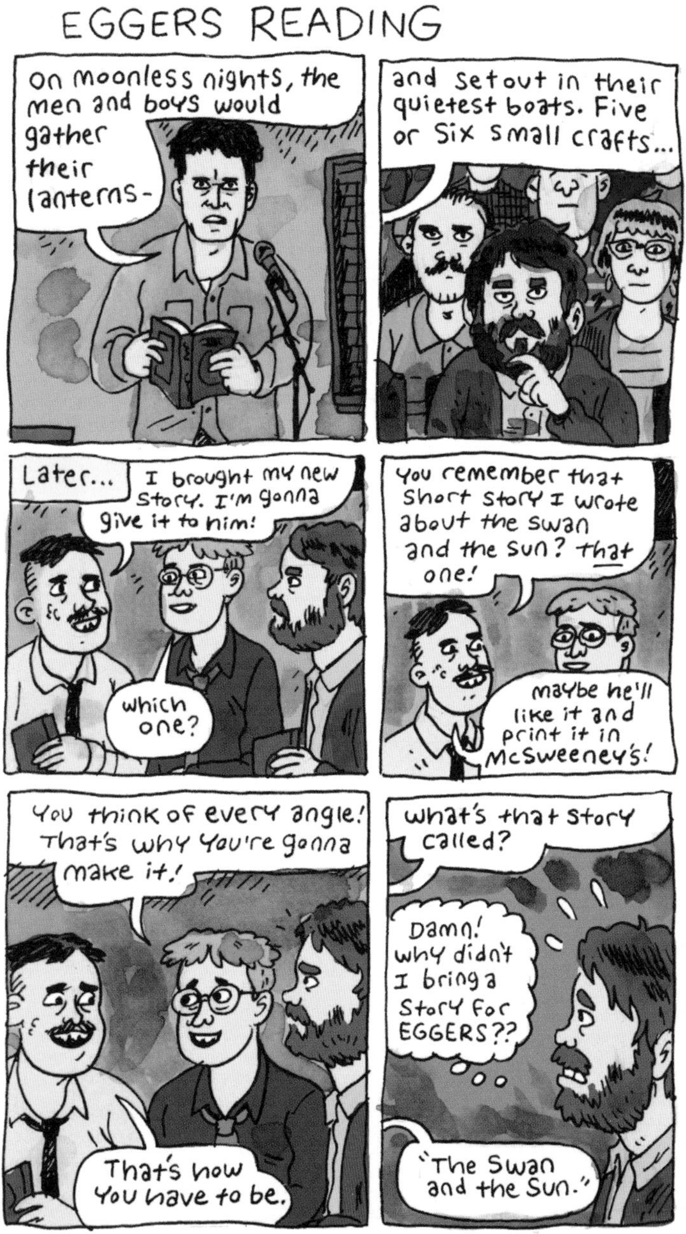
EGGERS READING
On moonless nights, the men and boys would gather their lanterns-
and set out in their quietest boats. Five or six small crafts...
Later...
I brought my new story. I'm gonna give it to him!
which one?
You remember that short story I wrote about the swan and the sun? that one!
maybe he'll like it and print it in McSweeney's!
You think of every angle! That's why you're gonna make it!
That's how you have to be.
What's that story called?
Damn! why didn't I bring a story for EGGERS??
"The Swan and the Sun."

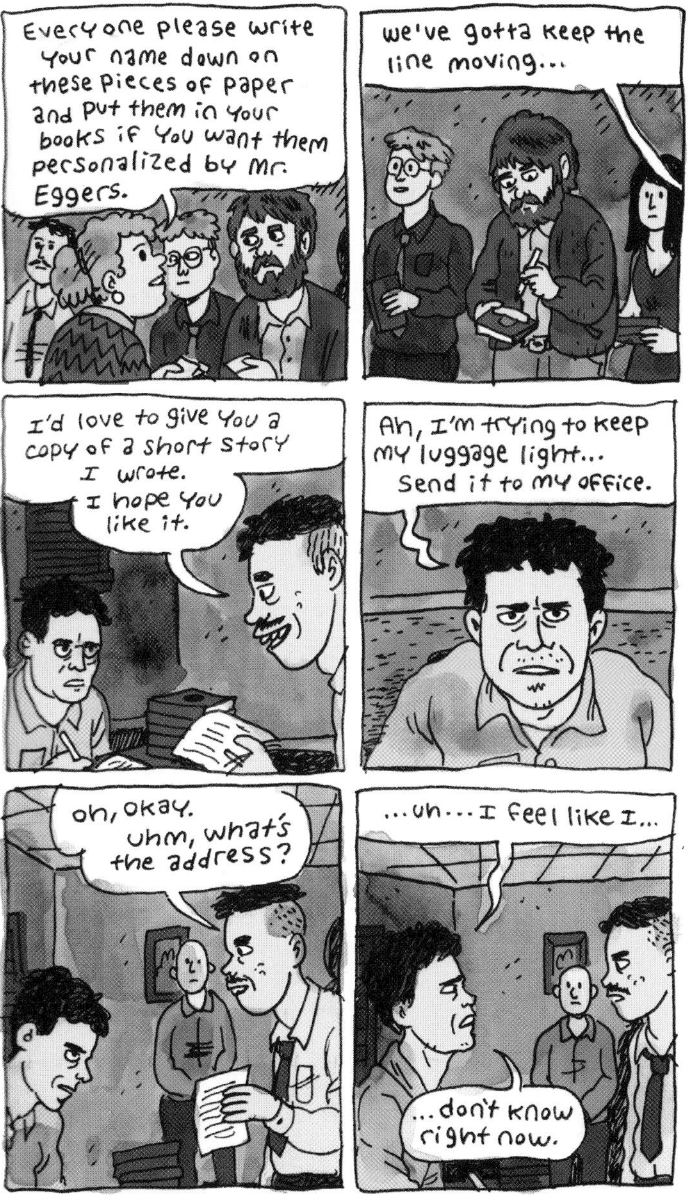
Everyone please write your name down on these pieces of paper and put them in your books if you want them personalized by Mr. Eggers.
we've gotta keep the line moving...
I'd love to give you a copy of a short story I wrote.
I hope you like it.
Ah, I'm trying to keep my luggage light... Send it to my office.
oh, okay.
uhm, what's the address?
...uh...I feel like I...
...don't know right now.

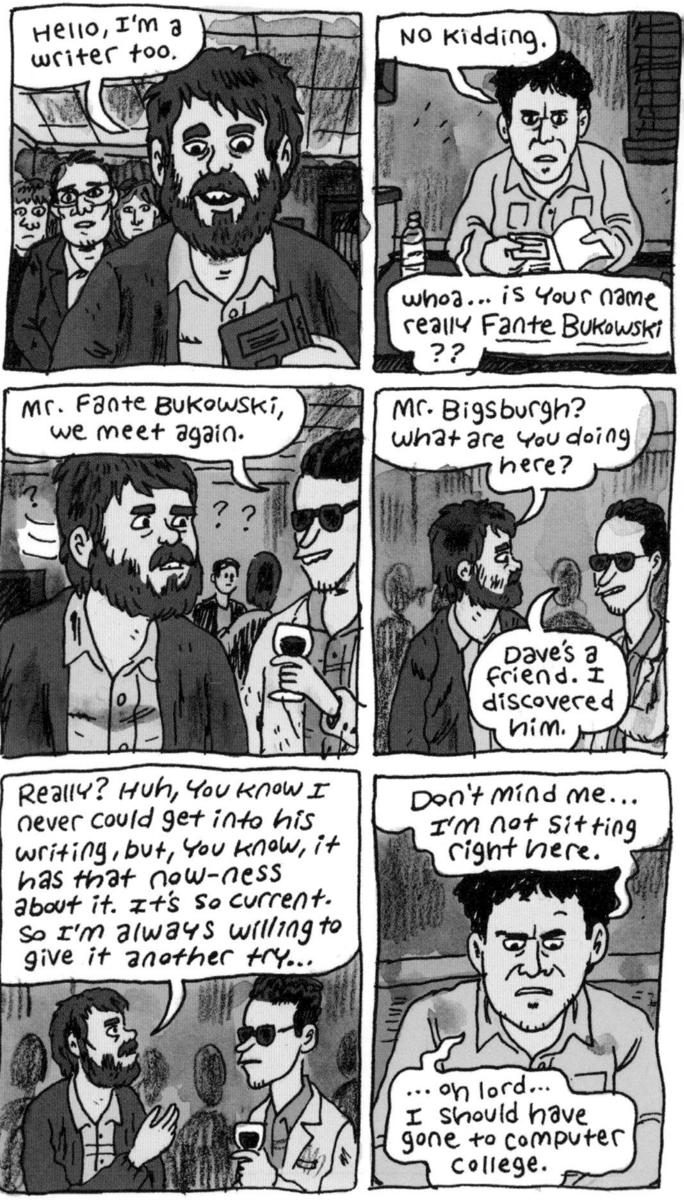
Hello, I'm a writer too.
No kidding.
whoa... is your name really Fante Bukowski ??
Mr. Fante Bukowski, we meet again.
? ? ?
Mr. Bigsburgh? what are you doing here?
Dave's a friend. I discovered him.
Really? Huh, you know I never could get into his writing, but, you know, it has that now-ness about it. It's so current. So I'm always willing to give it another try...
Don't mind me... I'm not sitting right here.
... oh lord... I should have gone to computer college.

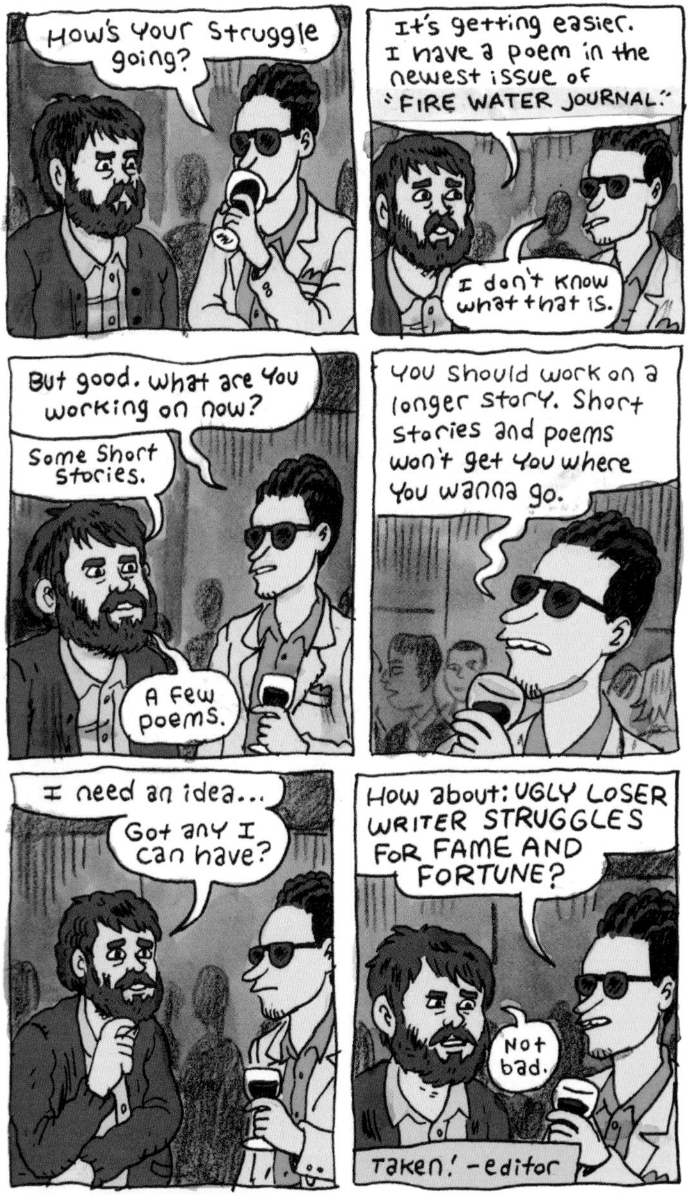
How's your struggle going?
It's getting easier. I have a poem in the newest issue of "FIRE WATER JOURNAL."
I don't know what that is.
But good. What are you working on now?
Some short stories.
A few poems.
You should work on a longer story. Short stories and poems won't get you where you wanna go.
I need an idea...
Got any I can have?
How about: UGLY LOSER WRITER STRUGGLES FOR FAME AND FORTUNE?
Not bad.
Taken! -editor

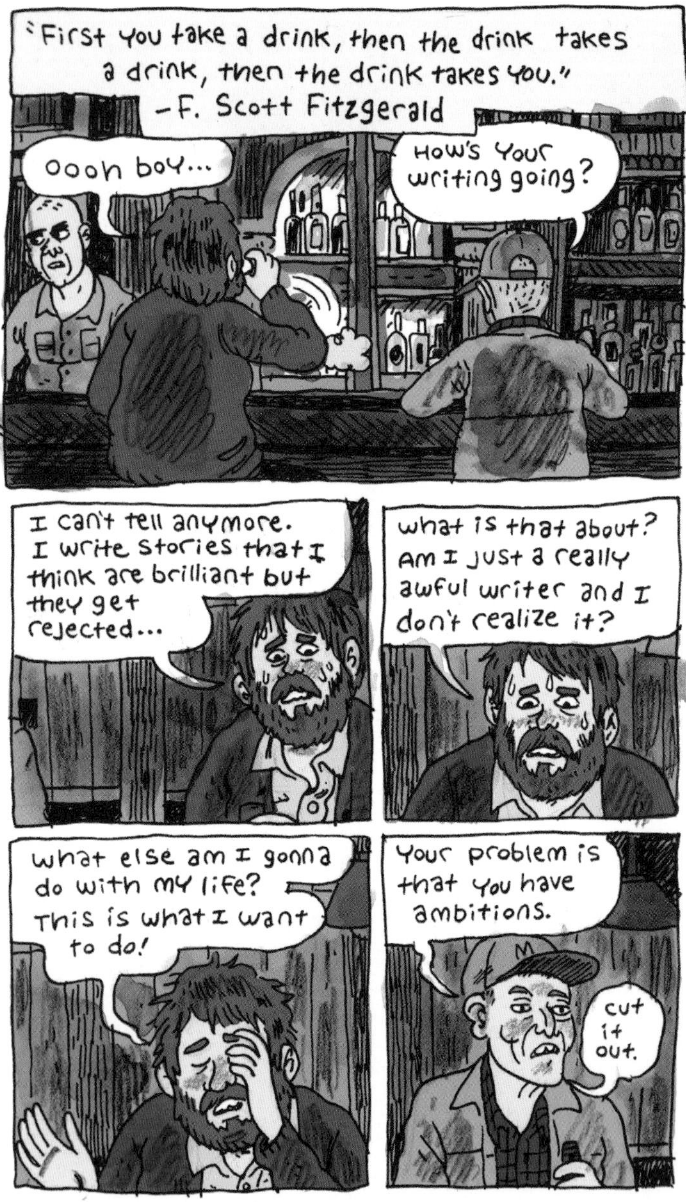
"First you take a drink, then the drink takes a drink, then the drink takes you." -F. Scott Fitzgerald
Oooh boy...
How's your writing going?
I can't tell anymore. I write stories that I think are brilliant but they get rejected...
What is that about? Am I just a really awful writer and I don't realize it?
What else am I gonna do with my life? This is what I want to do!
Your problem is that you have ambitions.
Cut it out.

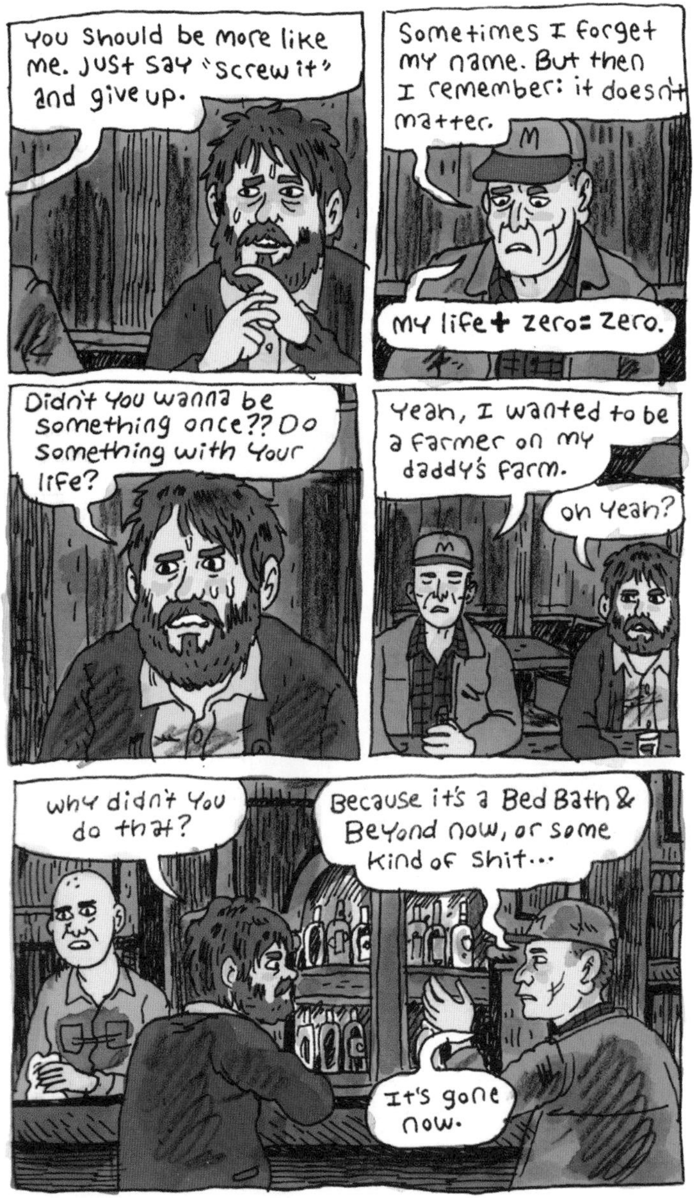
You should be more like me. Just say "screw it" and give up.
Sometimes I forget my name. But then I remember: it doesn't matter.
My life + zero = zero.
Didn't you wanna be something once?? Do something with your life?
Yeah, I wanted to be a farmer on my daddy's farm.
Oh yeah?
Why didn't you do that?
Because it's a Bed Bath & Beyond now, or some kind of shit...
It's gone now.

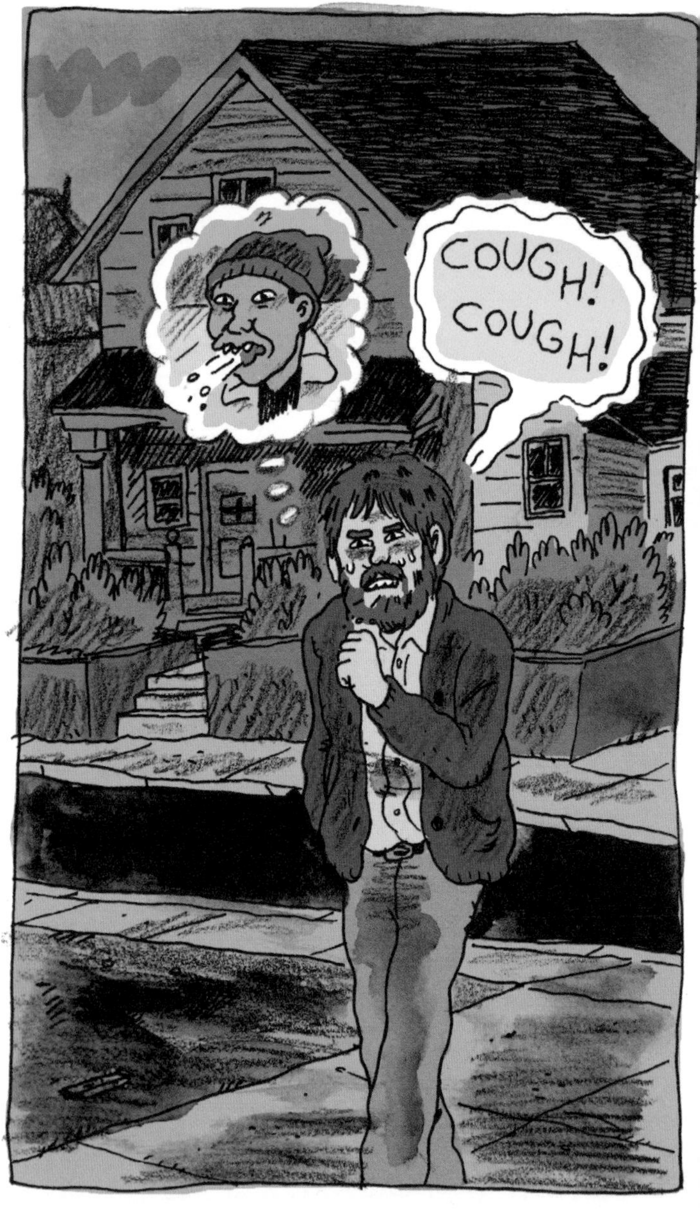
COUGH! COUGH!

FANTE HAS A FEVER

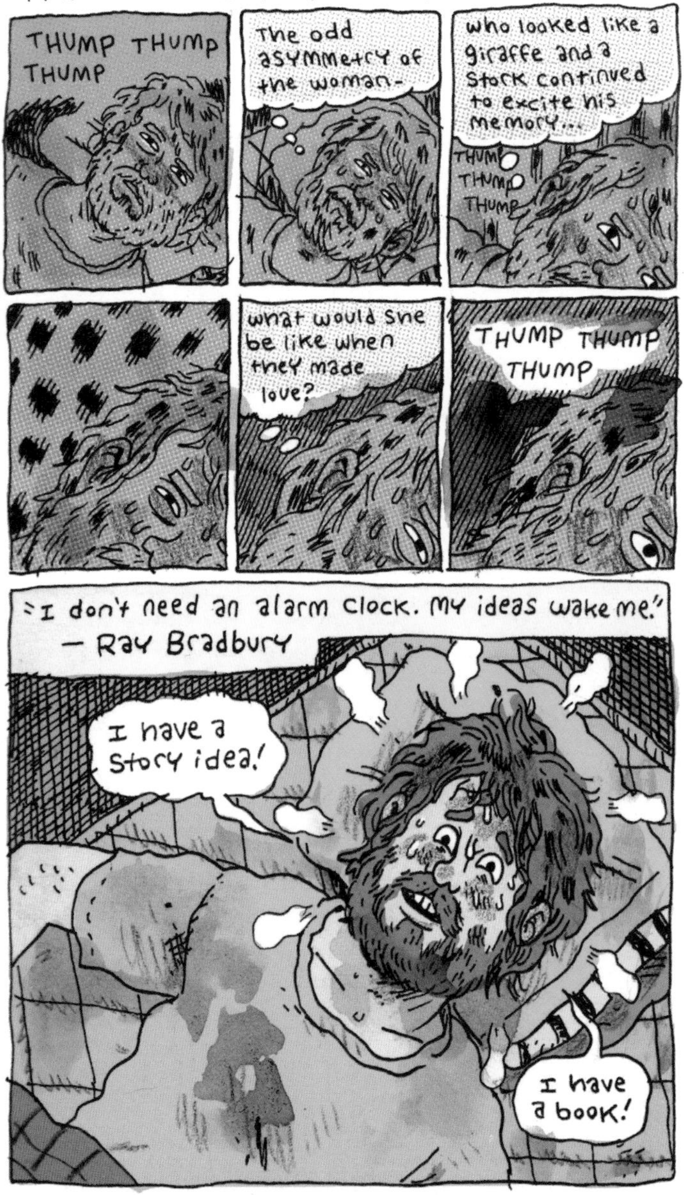

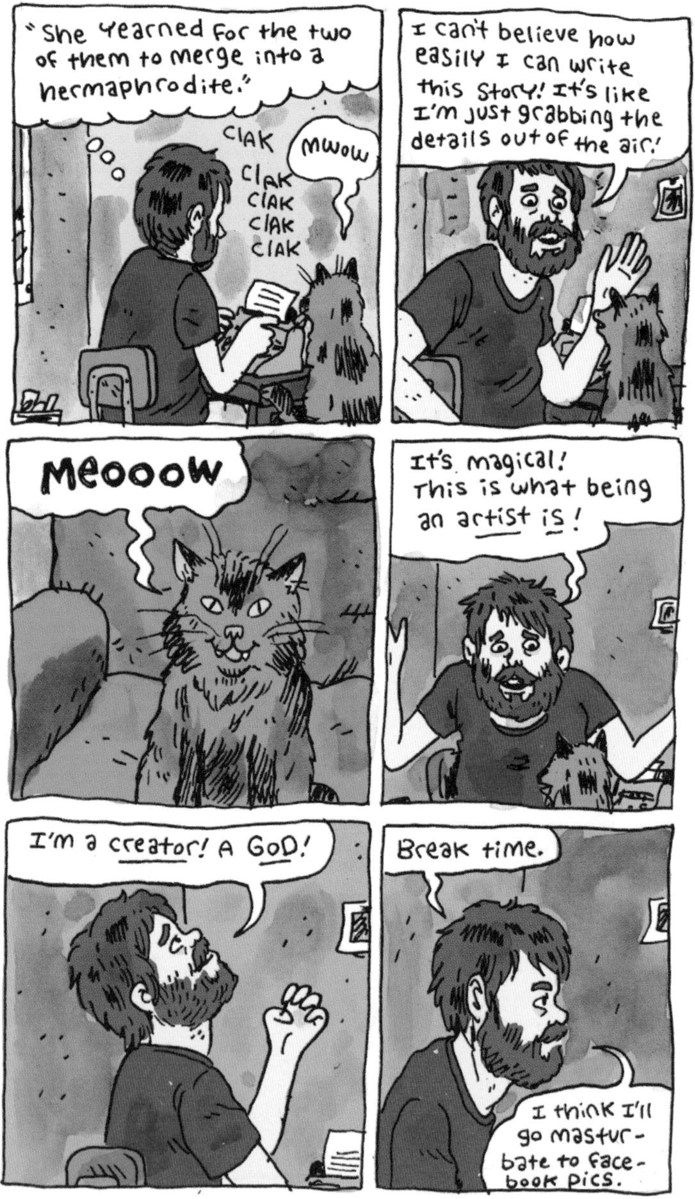
"She yearned for the two of them to merge into a hermaphrodite."
CLAK
MWOW
CLAK
CLAK
CLAK
CLAK
I can't believe how easily I can write this story! It's like I'm just grabbing the details out of the air!
Meooow
It's magical! This is what being an artist is!
I'm a creator! A GOD!
Break time.
I think I'll go mastur-bate to face-book pics.

POETRY READING

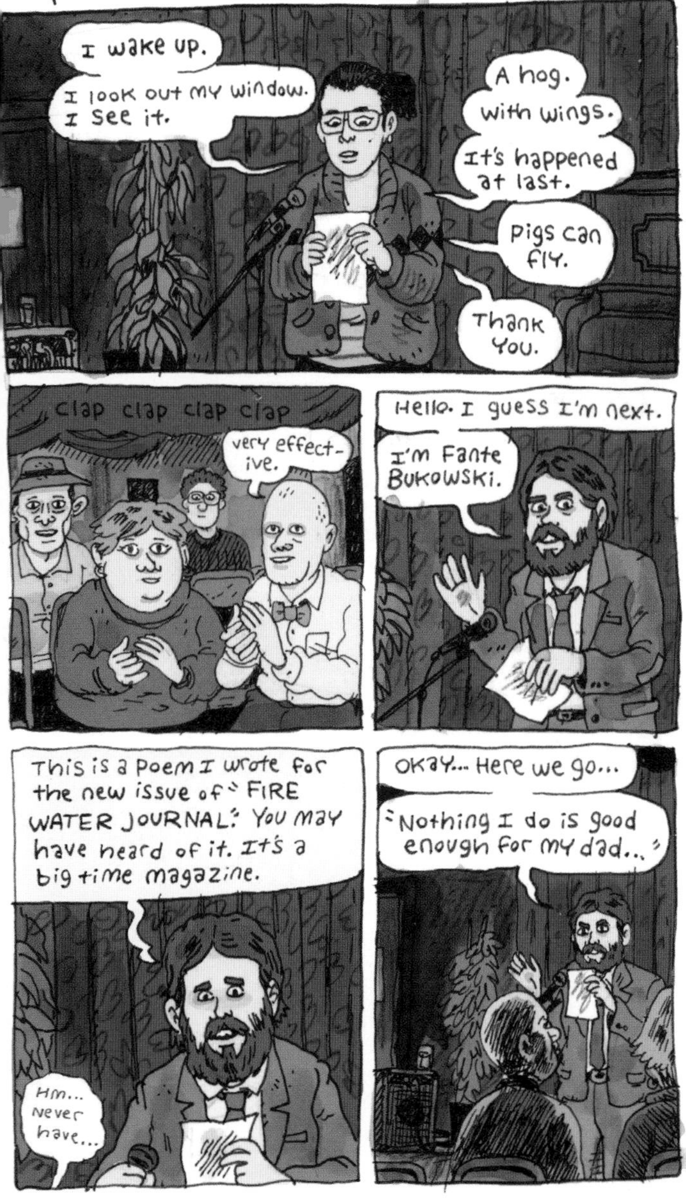

I wake up.
I look out my window. I see it.
A hog.
with wings.
It's happened at last.
Pigs can fly.
Thank You.
clap clap clap clap
very effect-ive.
Hello. I guess I'm next.
I'm Fante Bukowski.
This is a poem I wrote for the new issue of "FIRE WATER JOURNAL." You may have heard of it. It's a big time magazine.
Hm... Never have...
OKAY... Here we go...
"Nothing I do is good enough for my dad..."

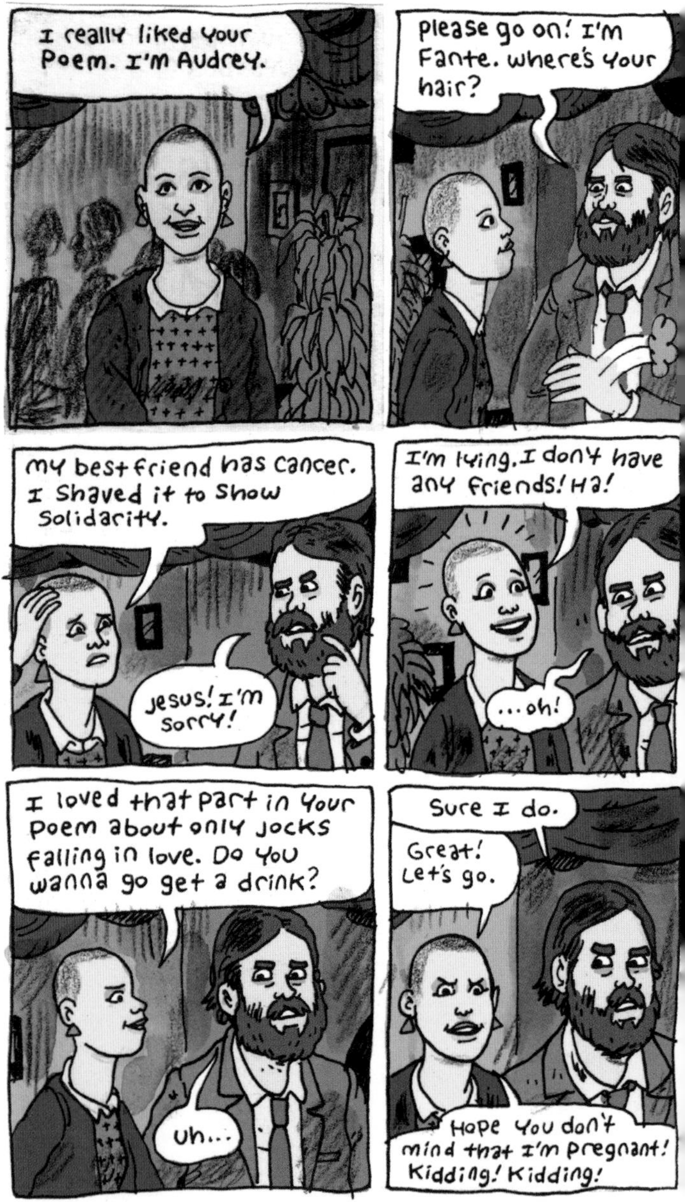
I really liked your Poem. I'm Audrey.
Please go on! I'm Fante. Where's your hair?
My best friend has cancer. I shaved it to show solidarity.
Jesus! I'm sorry!
I'm lying. I don't have any friends! Ha!
...oh!
I loved that part in your poem about only jocks falling in love. Do you wanna go get a drink?
uh...
Sure I do.
Great! Let's go.
Hope you don't mind that I'm pregnant! Kidding! Kidding!

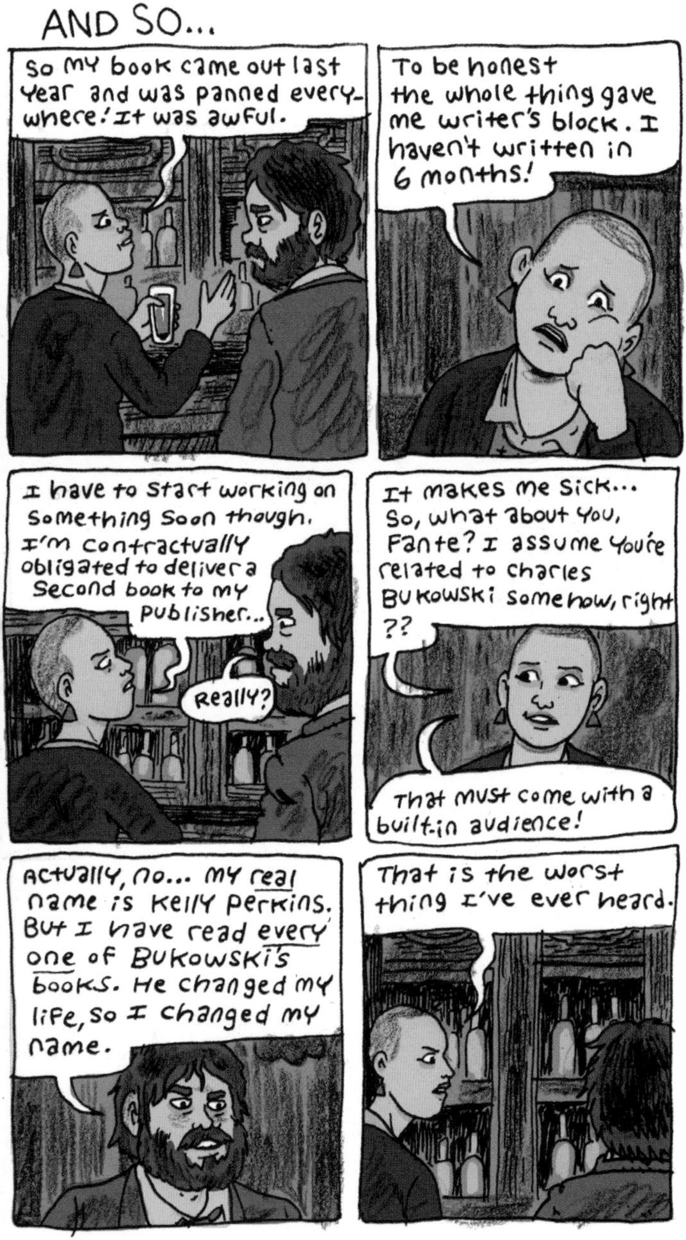

AND SO...
So my book came out last year and was panned every-where! It was awful.
To be honest the whole thing gave me writer's block. I haven't written in 6 months!
I have to start working on something soon though. I'm contractually obligated to deliver a second book to my publisher...
Really?
It makes me sick... So, what about you, Fante? I assume you're related to Charles Bukowski somehow, right??
That must come with a built-in audience!
Actually, no... my real name is Kelly Perkins. But I have read every one of Bukowski's books. He changed my life, so I changed my name.
That is the worst thing I've ever heard.

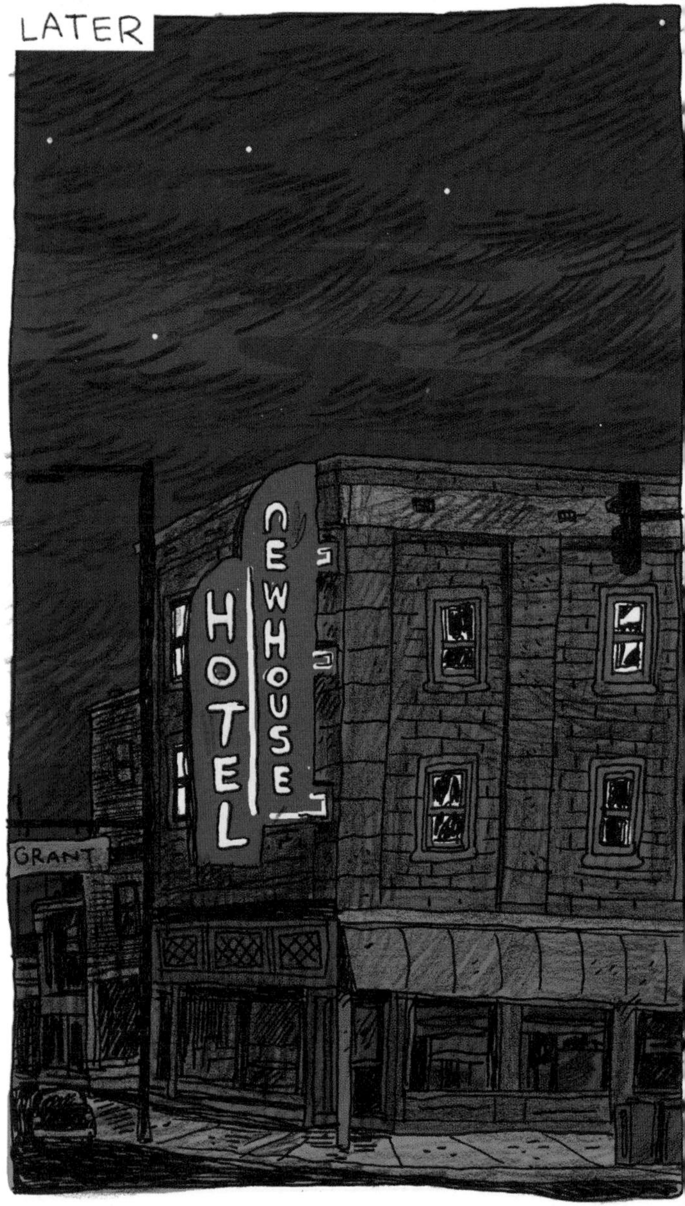
LATER
HOTEL
NEWHOUSE
GRANT

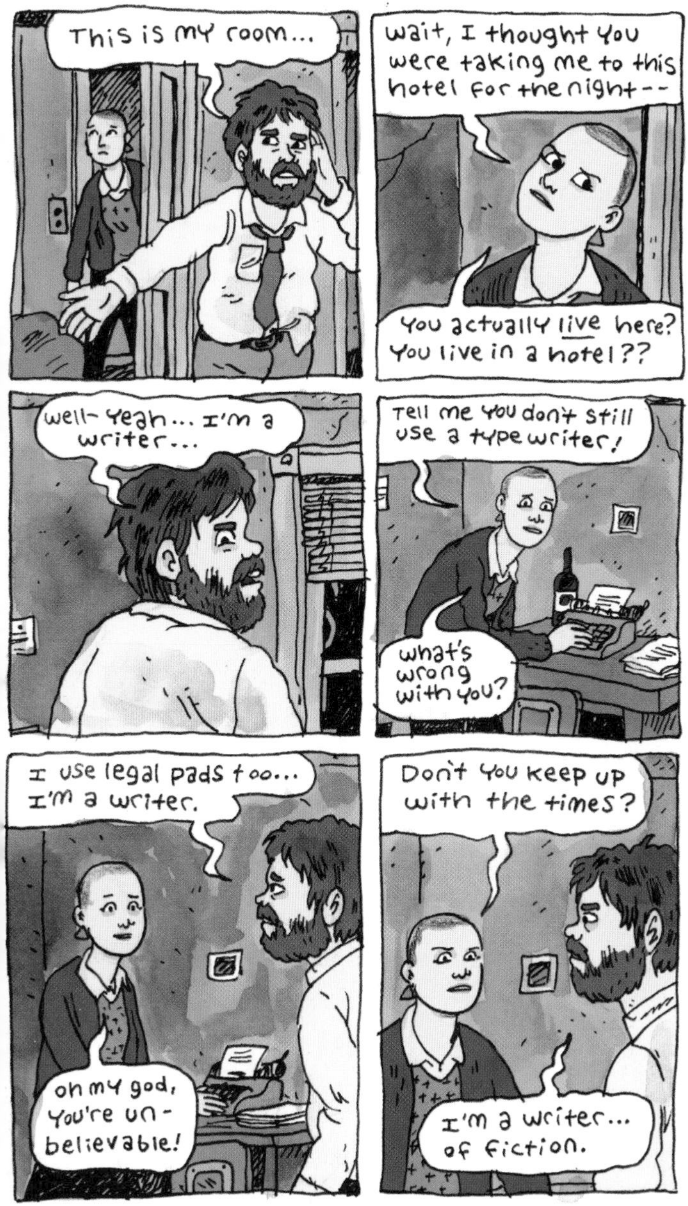
This is my room...
wait, I thought you were taking me to this hotel for the night--
You actually live here? You live in a hotel??
well- yeah... I'm a writer...
Tell me you don't still use a typewriter!
what's wrong with you?
I use legal pads too... I'm a writer.
oh my god, you're un-believable!
Don't you keep up with the times?
I'm a writer... of fiction.

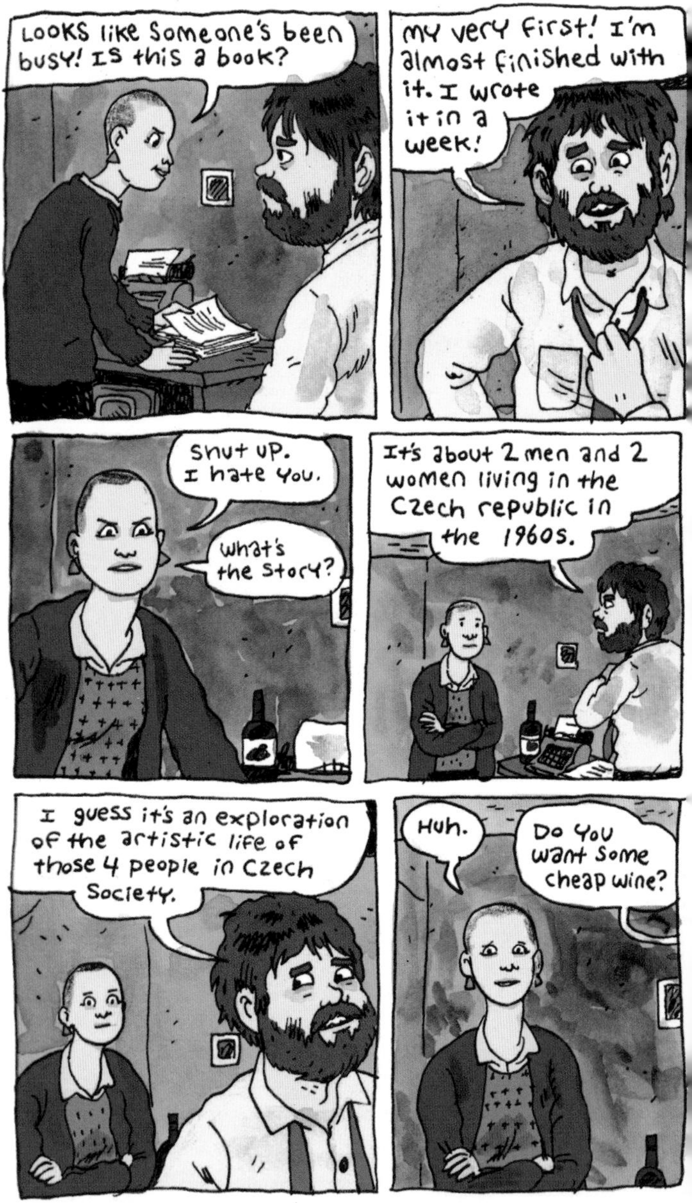
LOOKS like Someone's been busy! IS this a book?
my very first! I'm almost finished with it. I wrote it in a week!
Shut up. I hate you.
what's the Story?
It's about 2 men and 2 women living in the Czech republic in the 1960s.
I guess it's an exploration of the artistic life of those 4 people in Czech Society.
Huh.
Do you want some cheap wine?

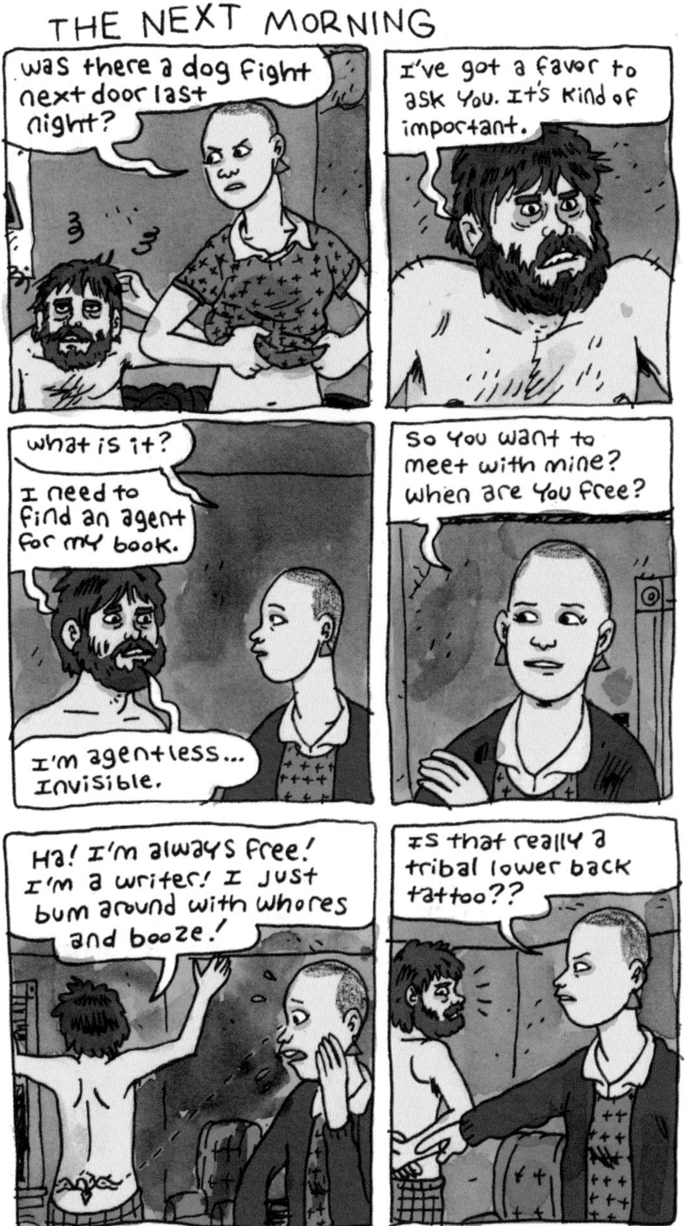
THE NEXT MORNING
was there a dog fight next door last night?
I've got a favor to ask you. It's kind of important.
what is it?
I need to find an agent for my book.
I'm agentless... Invisible.
So you want to meet with mine? when are you free?
Ha! I'm always free! I'm a writer! I just bum around with whores and booze!
Is that really a tribal lower back tattoo??

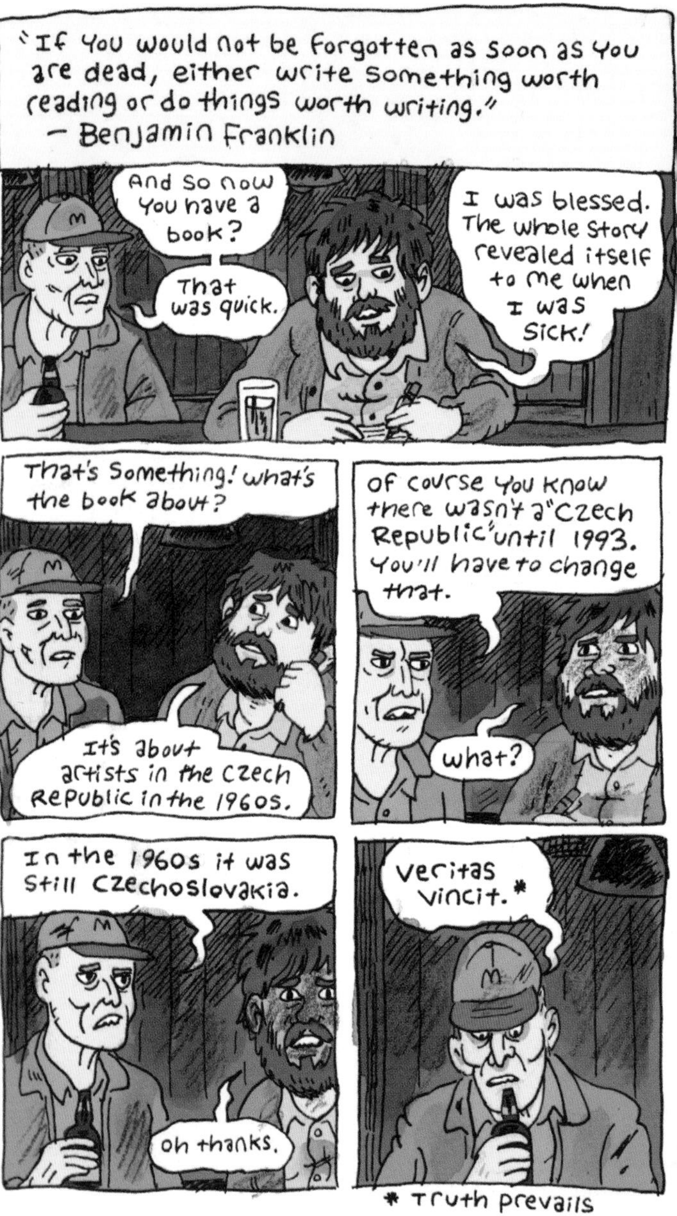
"If you would not be forgotten as soon as you are dead, either write something worth reading or do things worth writing." — Benjamin Franklin
And so now you have a book?
That was quick.
I was blessed. The whole story revealed itself to me when I was sick!
That's something! what's the book about?
It's about artists in the Czech Republic in the 1960s.
Of course you know there wasn't a "Czech Republic" until 1993. You'll have to change that.
what?
In the 1960s it was still Czechoslovakia.
oh thanks.
veritas vincit.*

* Truth prevails

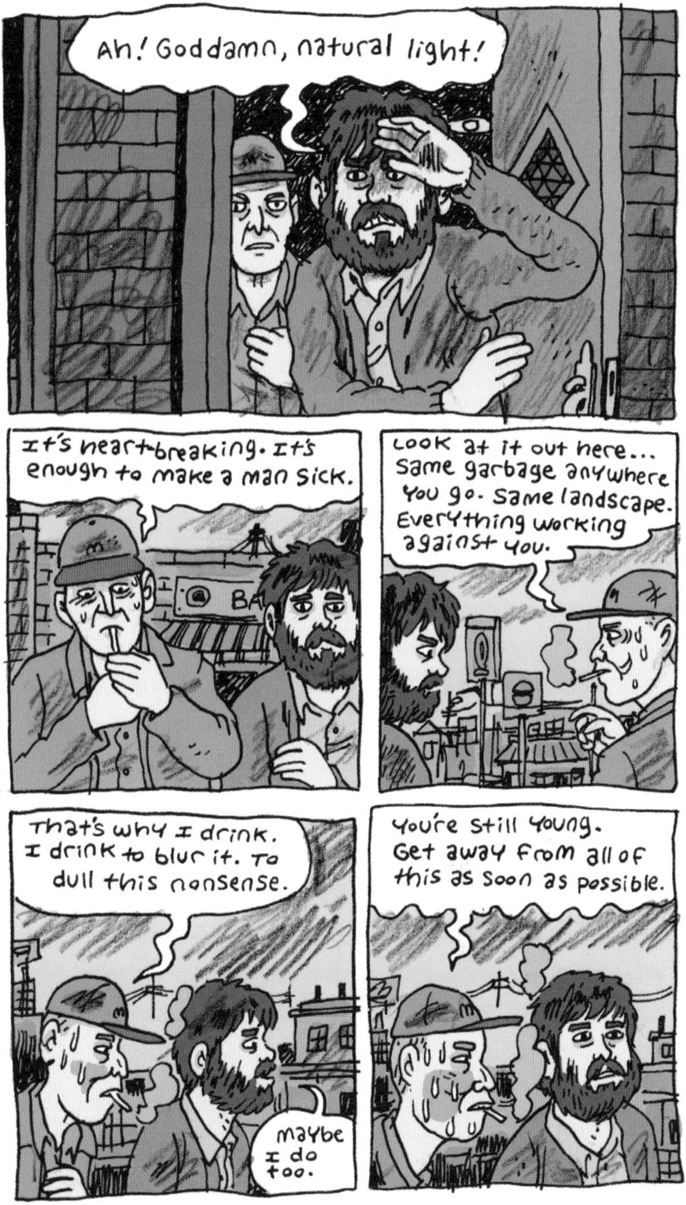
Ah! Goddamn, natural light!
It's heart-breaking. It's enough to make a man sick.
Look at it out here... Same garbage anywhere you go. Same landscape. Everything working against you.
That's why I drink. I drink to blur it. To dull this nonsense.
Maybe I do too.
You're still young. Get away from all of this as soon as possible.

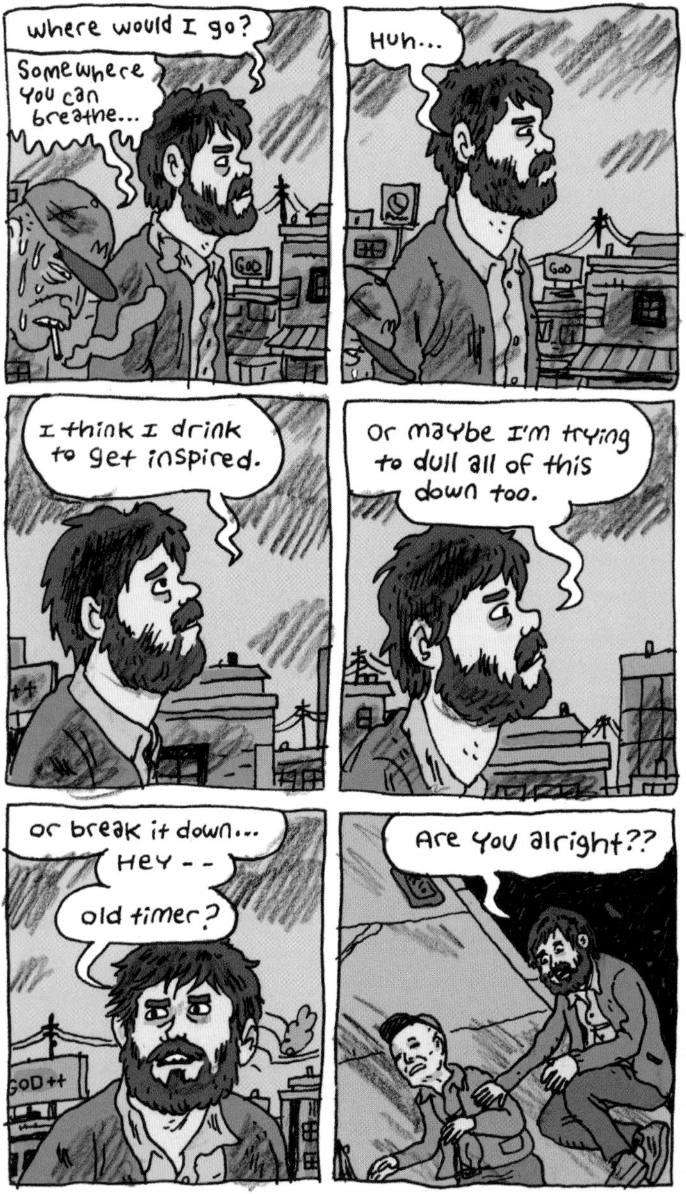
where would I go?
Somewhere you can breathe...
GOD
Huh...
GOD
I think I drink to get inspired.
Or maybe I'm trying to dull all of this down too.
or break it down...
HEY --
old timer?
GOD++
Are you alright??

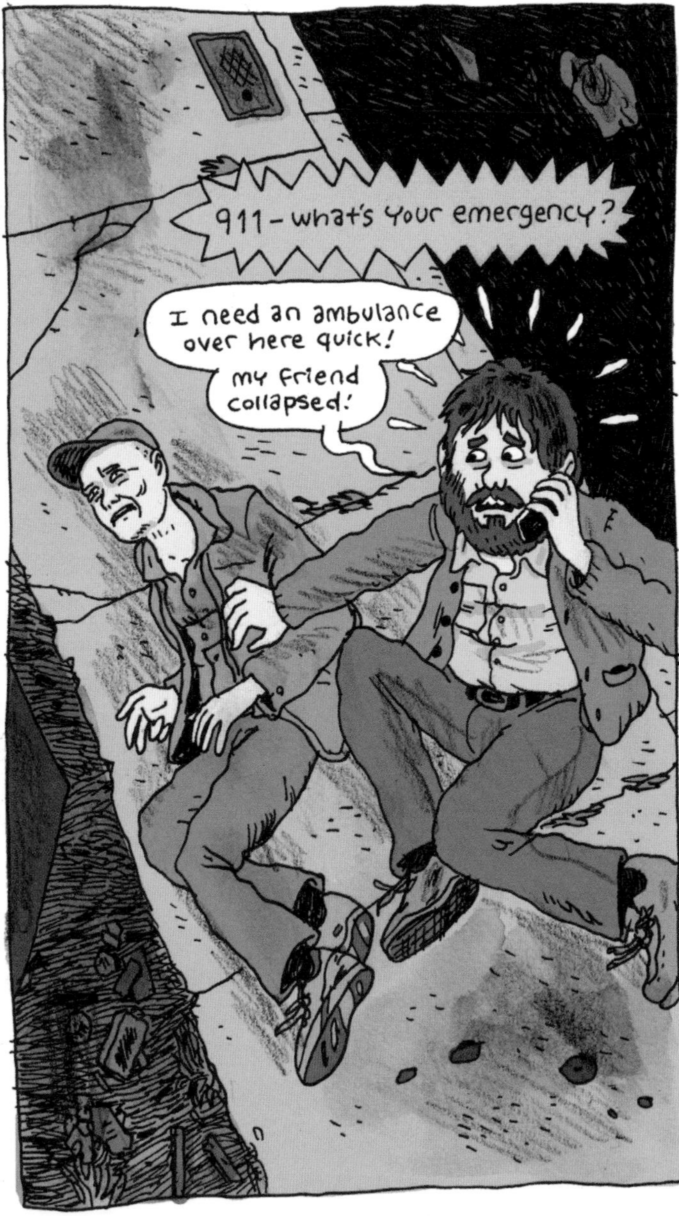
911 - what's your emergency?
I need an ambulance over here quick!
my friend collapsed!

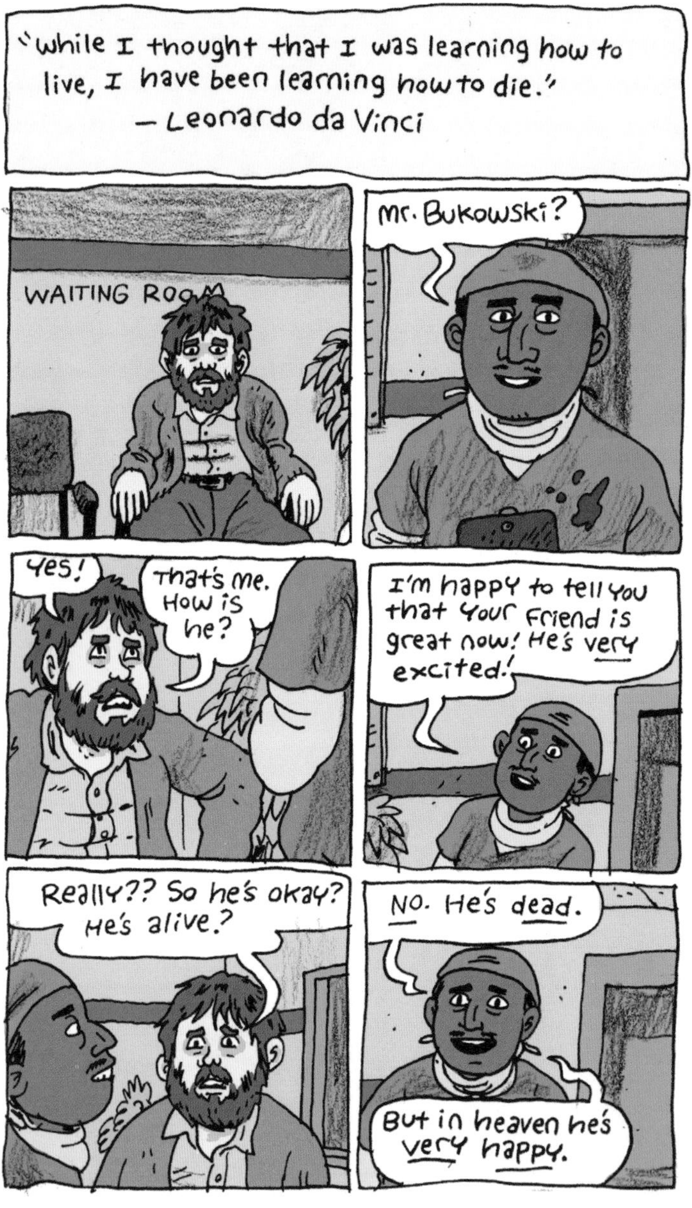
"while I thought that I was learning how to live, I have been learning how to die."
— Leonardo da Vinci
WAITING ROOM
Mr. Bukowski?
Yes!
That's me. How is he?
I'm happy to tell you that your friend is great now! He's very excited!
Really?? So he's okay? He's alive?
No. He's dead.
But in heaven he's very happy.

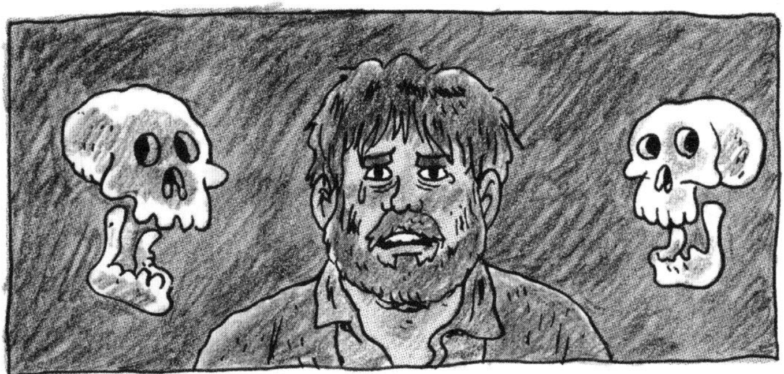

~~kelly perkins~~ Fante Bukowski wants an agent

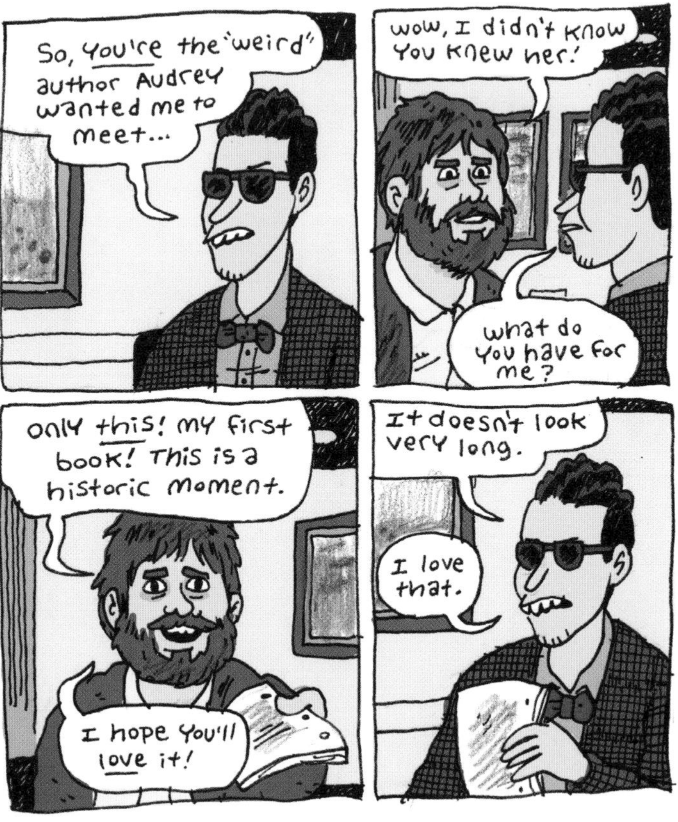

So, you're the "weird" author Audrey wanted me to meet...
wow, I didn't know you knew her!
what do you have for me?
only this! my first book! This is a historic moment.
I hope you'll love it!
It doesn't look very long.
I love that.

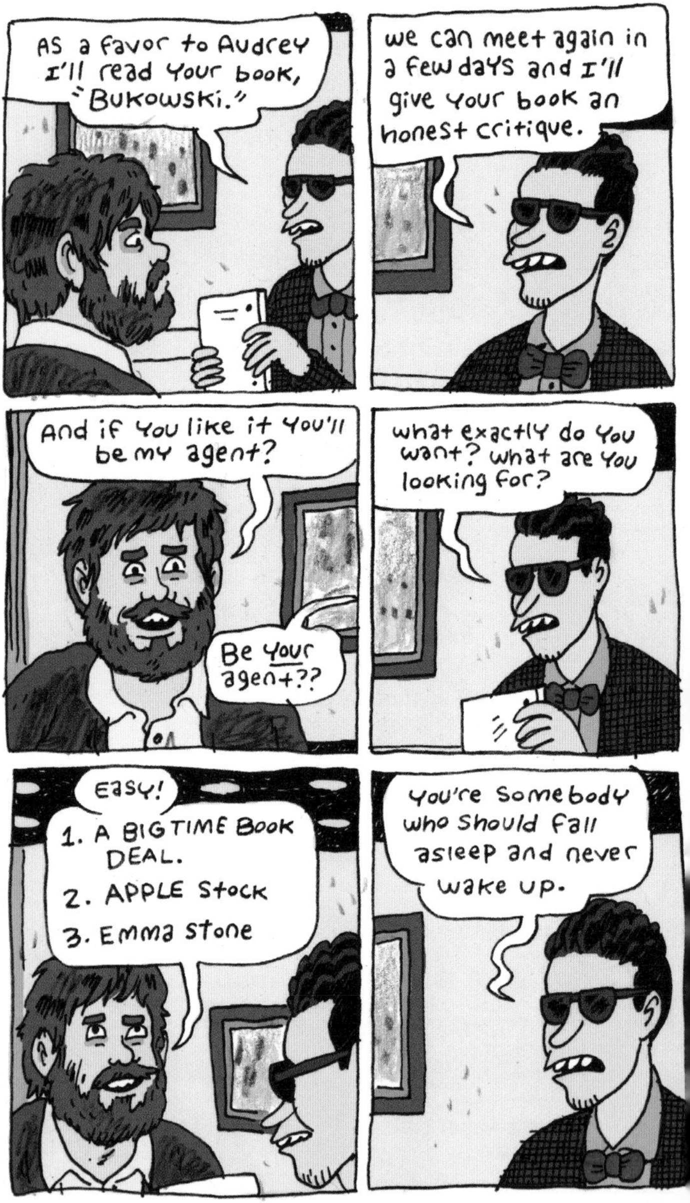
AS a favor to Audrey I'll read your book, "Bukowski."
we can meet again in a few days and I'll give your book an honest critique.
And if you like it you'll be my agent?
Be your agent??
what exactly do you want? what are you looking for?
Easy!
1. A BIGTIME Book DEAL.
2. APPLE Stock
3. Emma Stone
You're Somebody who should fall asleep and never wake up.

FANTE'S OLD FRIEND

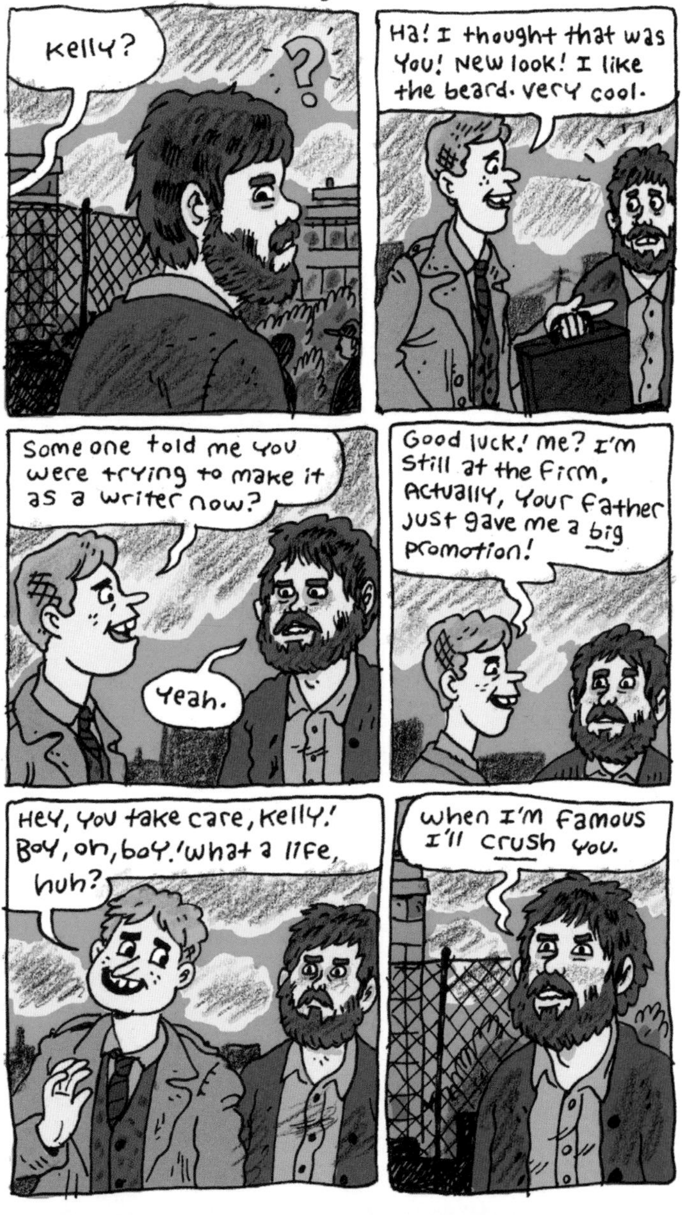
Kelly?
?
Ha! I thought that was you! New look! I like the beard. Very cool.
Some one told me you were trying to make it as a writer now?
Yeah.
Good luck! Me? I'm still at the firm. Actually, your father just gave me a big promotion!
Hey, you take care, Kelly! Boy, oh, boy! What a life, huh?
When I'm famous I'll crush you.

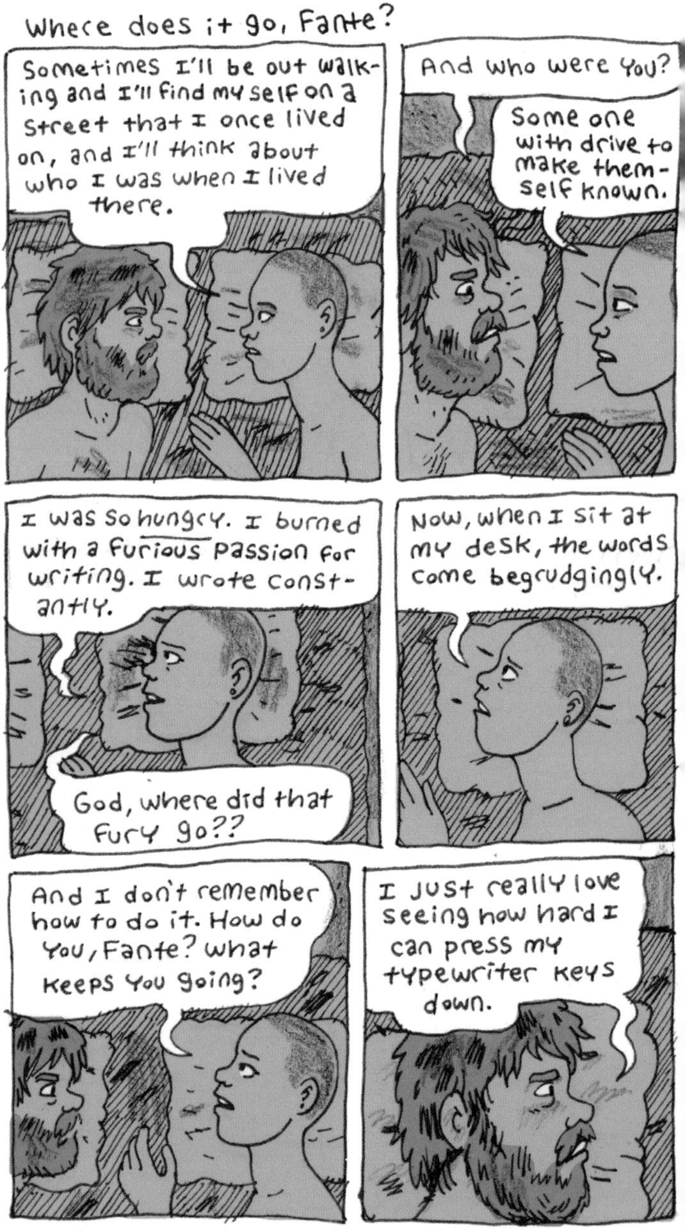
Where does it go, Fante?
Sometimes I'll be out walking and I'll find myself on a street that I once lived on, and I'll think about who I was when I lived there.
And who were you?
Some one with drive to make themself known.
I was so hungry. I burned with a furious passion for writing. I wrote constantly.
God, where did that fury go??
Now, when I sit at my desk, the words come begrudgingly.
And I don't remember how to do it. How do you, Fante? What keeps you going?
I just really love seeing how hard I can press my typewriter keys down.

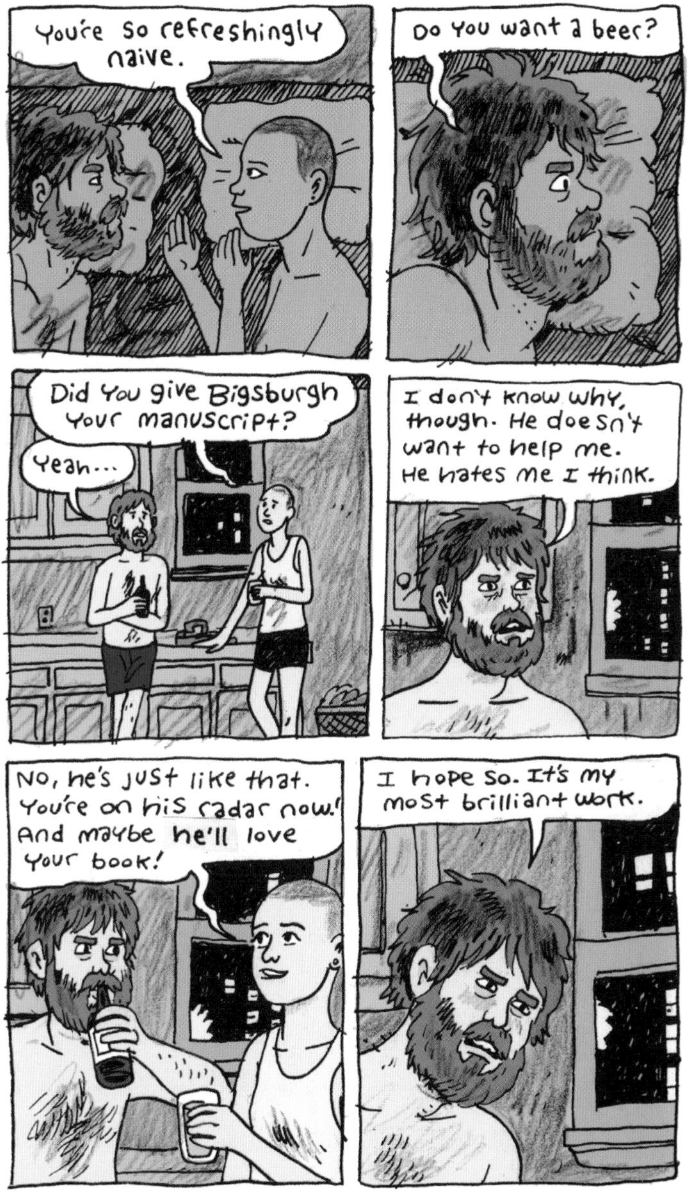
You're so refreshingly naive.
Do you want a beer?
Did you give Bigsburgh your manuscript?
Yeah...
I don't know why, though. He doesn't want to help me. He hates me I think.
No, he's just like that. You're on his radar now! And maybe he'll love your book!
I hope so. It's my most brilliant work.

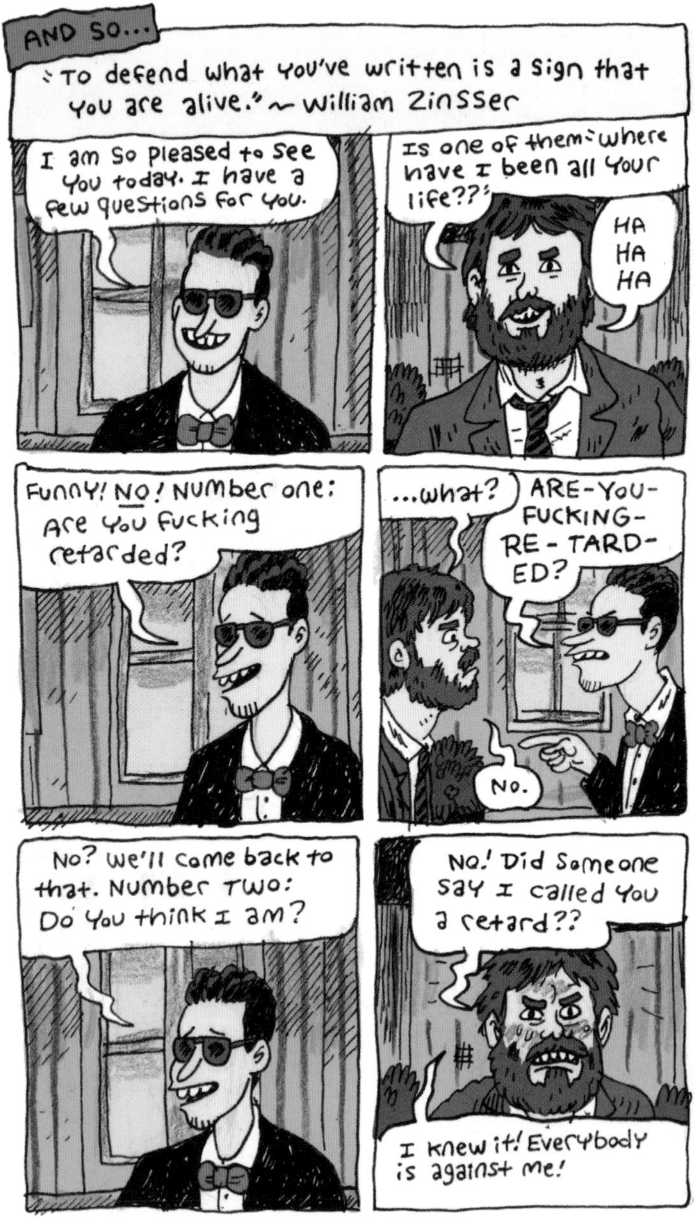
AND SO...
"To defend what you've written is a sign that you are alive." ~ William Zinsser
I am so pleased to see you today. I have a few questions for you.
Is one of them: "where have I been all your life??"
HA HA HA
Funny! NO! Number one: Are you fucking retarded?
...what?
ARE-YOU-FUCKING-RE-TARD-ED?
No.
No? We'll come back to that. Number two: Do you think I am?
No! Did someone say I called you a retard??
I knew it! Everybody is against me!

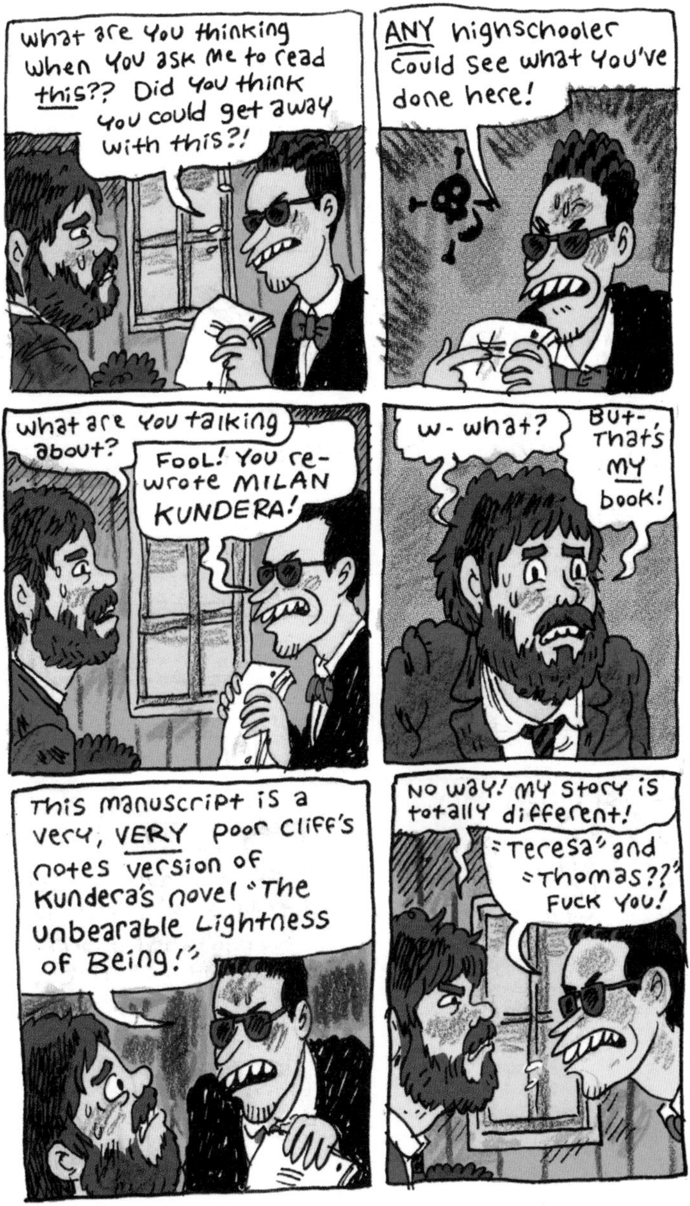
What are you thinking when you ask me to read this?? Did you think you could get away with this?!
ANY highschooler could see what you've done here!
What are you talking about?
Fool! You re-wrote MILAN KUNDERA!
W-what?
But-, That's MY book!
This manuscript is a very, VERY poor Cliff's notes version of Kundera's novel "The Unbearable Lightness of Being!"
No way! My story is totally different!
"Teresa" and "Thomas??" Fuck you!

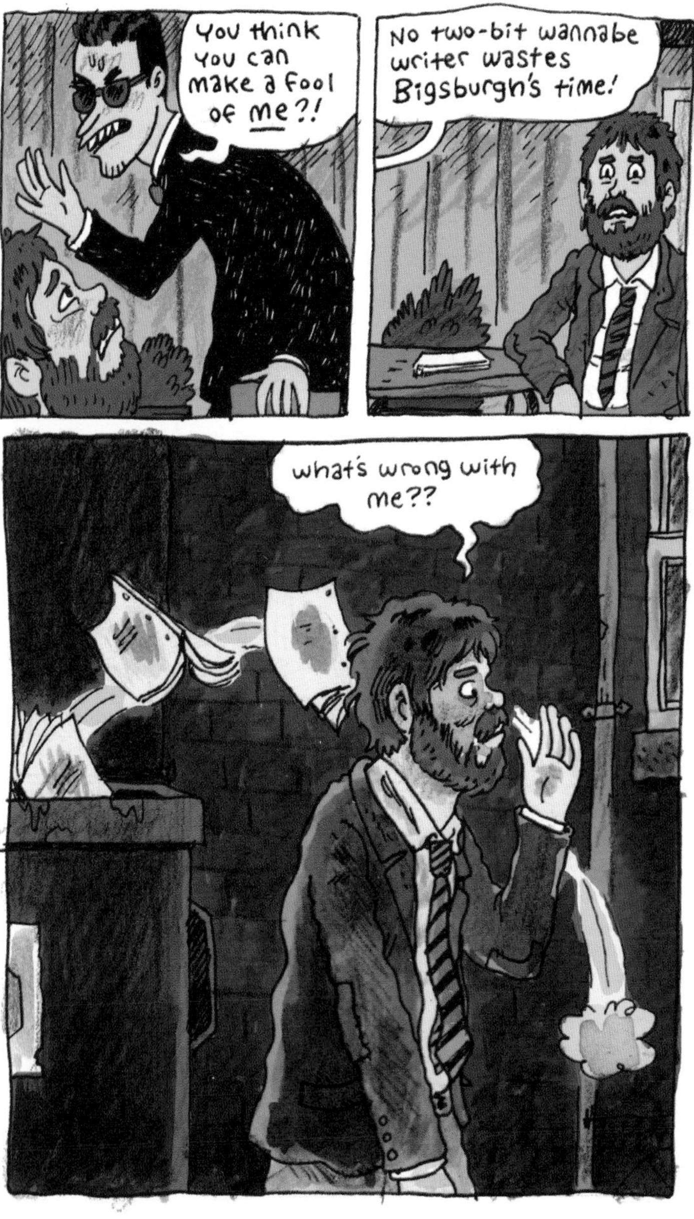
You think you can make a fool of me?!
No two-bit wannabe writer wastes Bigsburgh's time!
what's wrong with me??

INVASION OF THE JOCKS

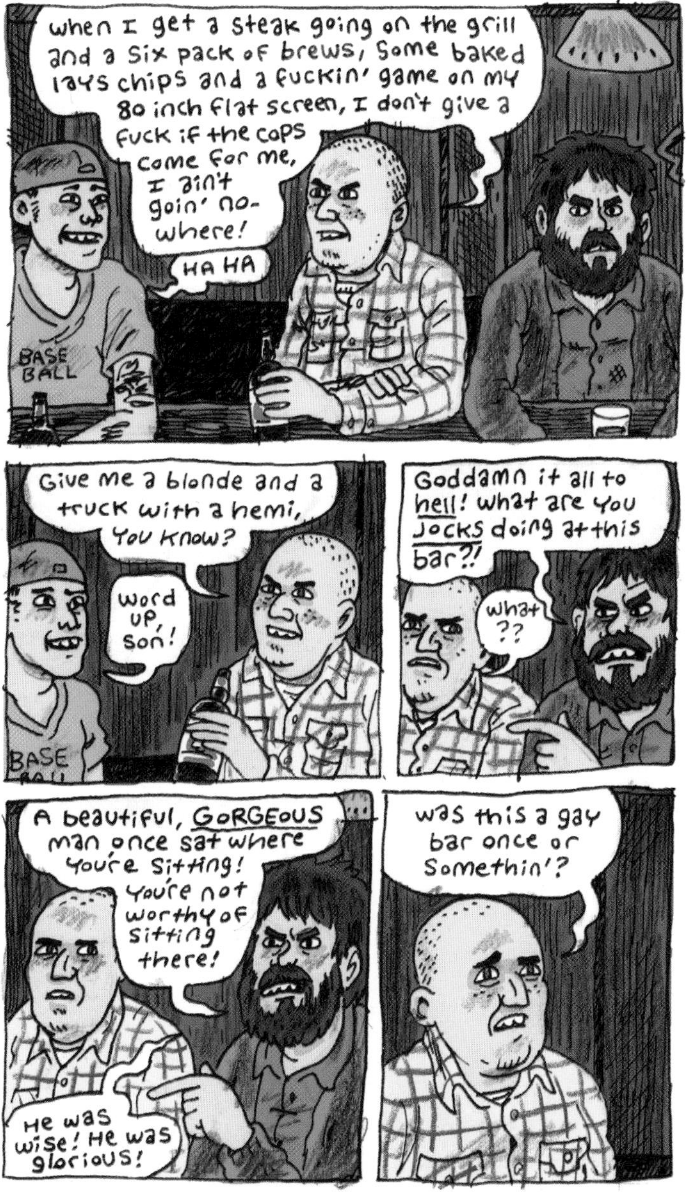
when I get a steak going on the grill and a six pack of brews, some baked lays chips and a fuckin' game on my 80 inch flat screen, I don't give a fuck if the cops come for me, I ain't goin' no-where!
HA HA
Give me a blonde and a truck with a hemi, You know?
word up, son!
Goddamn it all to hell! what are you JOCKS doing at this bar?!
what ??
A beautiful, GORGEOUS man once sat where you're sitting! You're not worthy of sitting there!
He was wise! He was glorious!
was this a gay bar once or somethin'?
BASE BALL

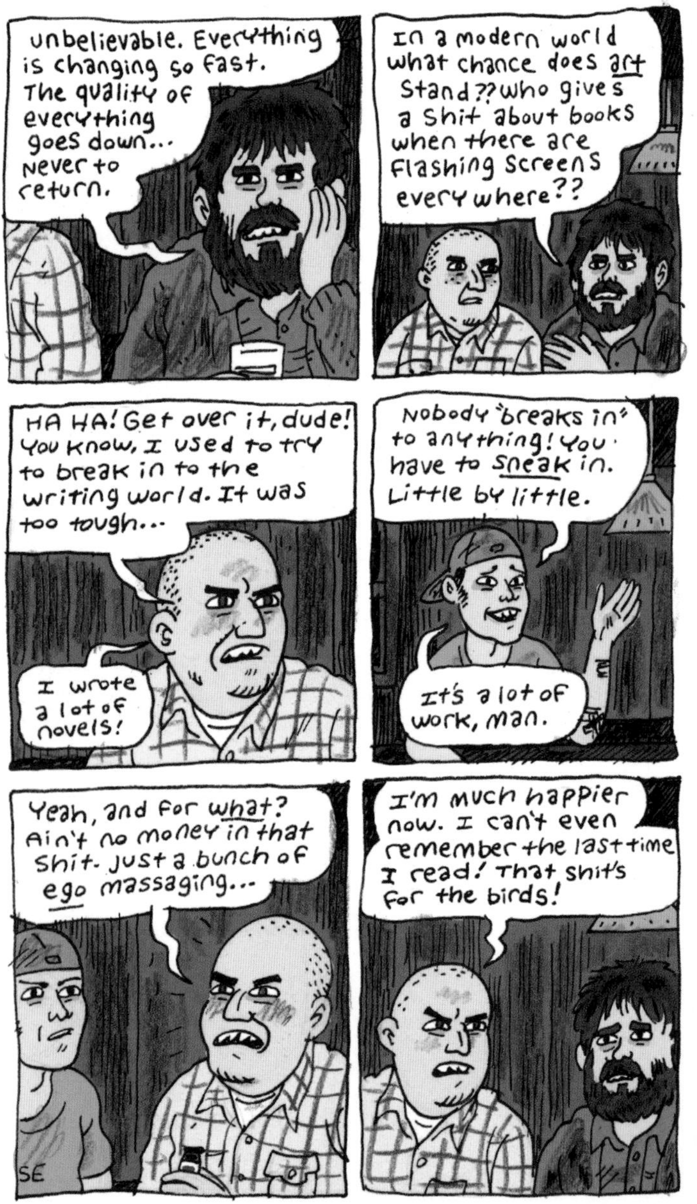
unbelievable. Everything is changing so fast. The quality of everything goes down... never to return.
In a modern world what chance does art stand?? who gives a shit about books when there are flashing screens everywhere??
HA HA! Get over it, dude! You know, I used to try to break in to the writing world. It was too tough...
I wrote a lot of novels!
Nobody "breaks in" to anything! You have to sneak in. Little by little.
It's a lot of work, man.
Yeah, and for what? Ain't no money in that shit. Just a bunch of ego massaging...
I'm much happier now. I can't even remember the last time I read! That shit's for the birds!
SE

FANTE COULD CRY

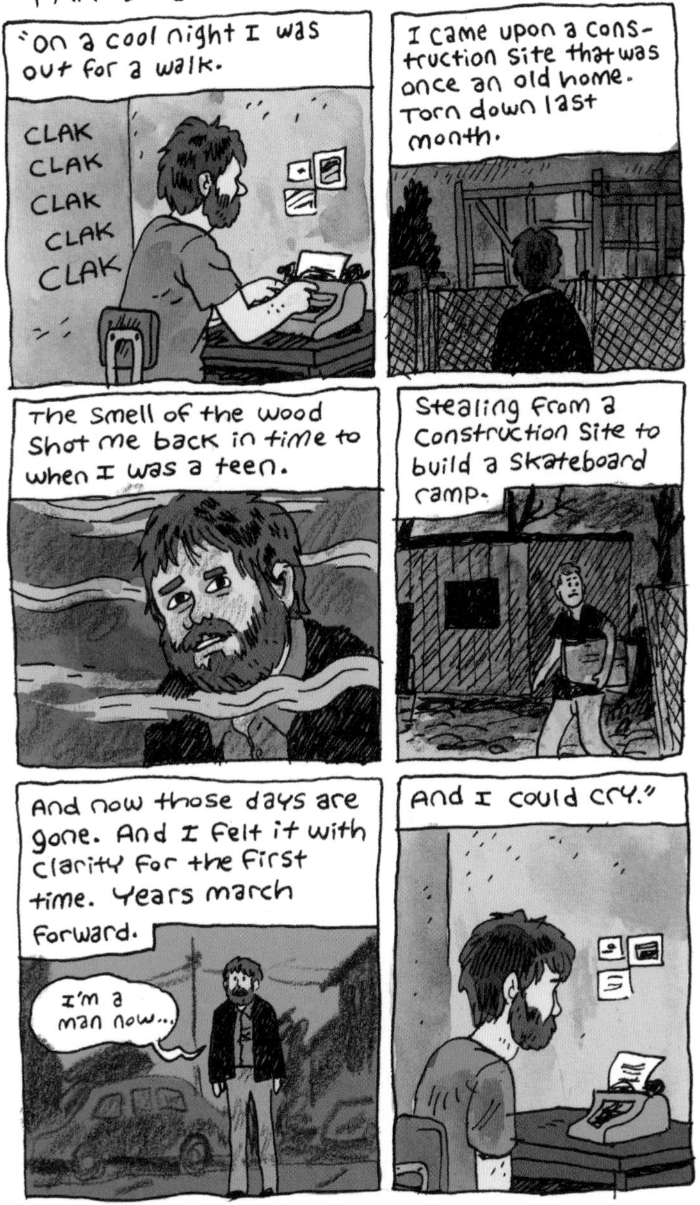
"On a cool night I was out for a walk.
CLAK CLAK CLAK CLAK CLAK
I came upon a construction site that was once an old home. Torn down last month.
The smell of the wood shot me back in time to when I was a teen.
Stealing from a construction site to build a skateboard ramp.
And now those days are gone. And I felt it with clarity for the first time. Years march forward.
I'm a man now...
And I could cry."

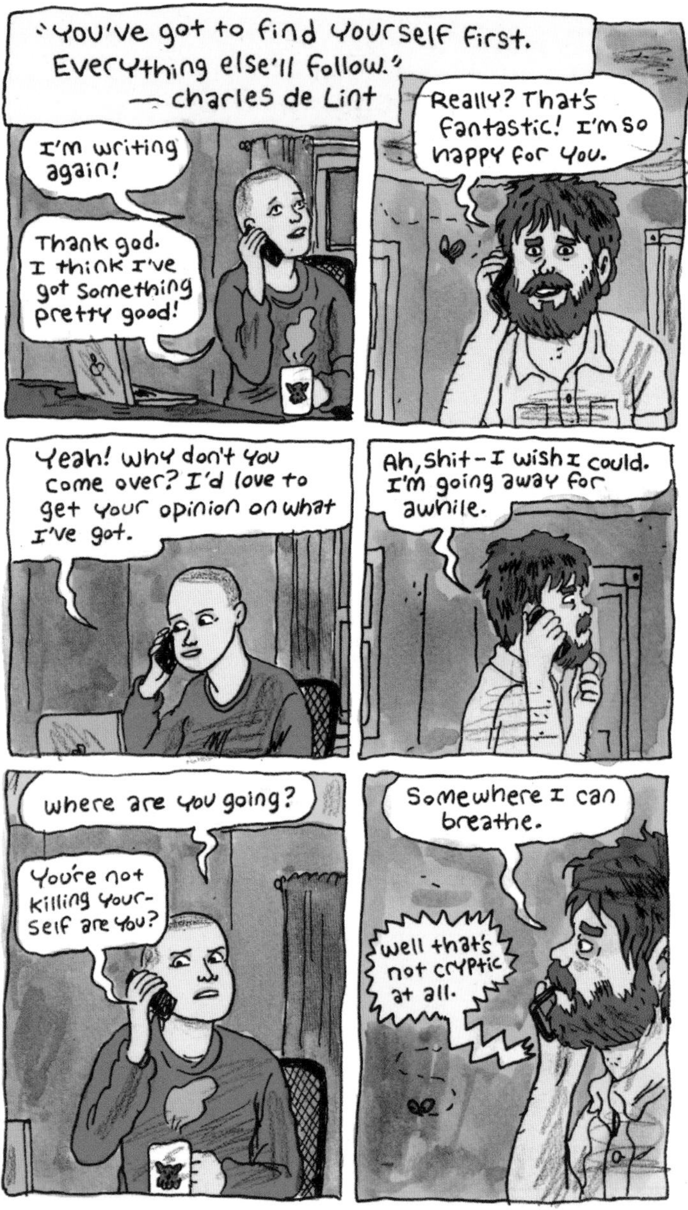
"You've got to find yourself first. Everything else'll follow."
—charles de Lint
I'm writing again!
Thank god. I think I've got something pretty good!
Really? That's fantastic! I'm so happy for you.
Yeah! why don't you come over? I'd love to get your opinion on what I've got.
Ah, shit - I wish I could. I'm going away for awhile.
where are you going?
You're not killing your-self are you?
Somewhere I can breathe.
well that's not cryptic at all.

FANTE BIDS FAREWELL

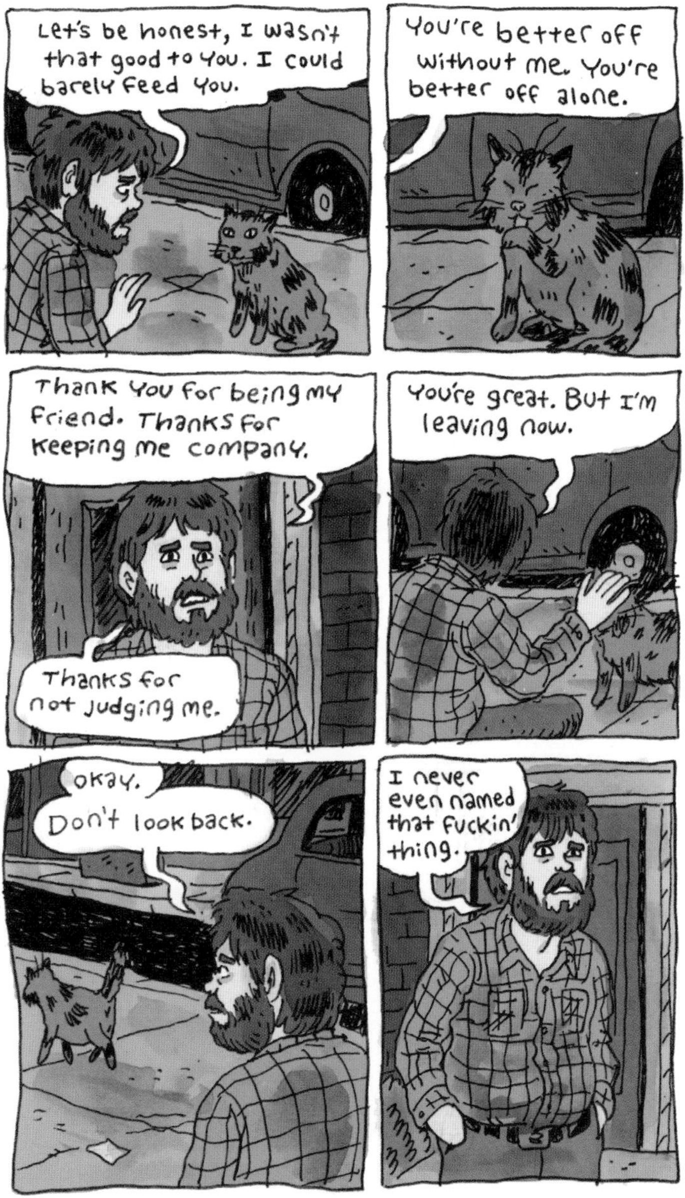
Let's be honest, I wasn't that good to you. I could barely feed you.
You're better off without me. You're better off alone.
Thank you for being my friend. Thanks for keeping me company.
Thanks for not judging me.
You're great. But I'm leaving now.
Okay.
Don't look back.
I never even named that fuckin' thing.

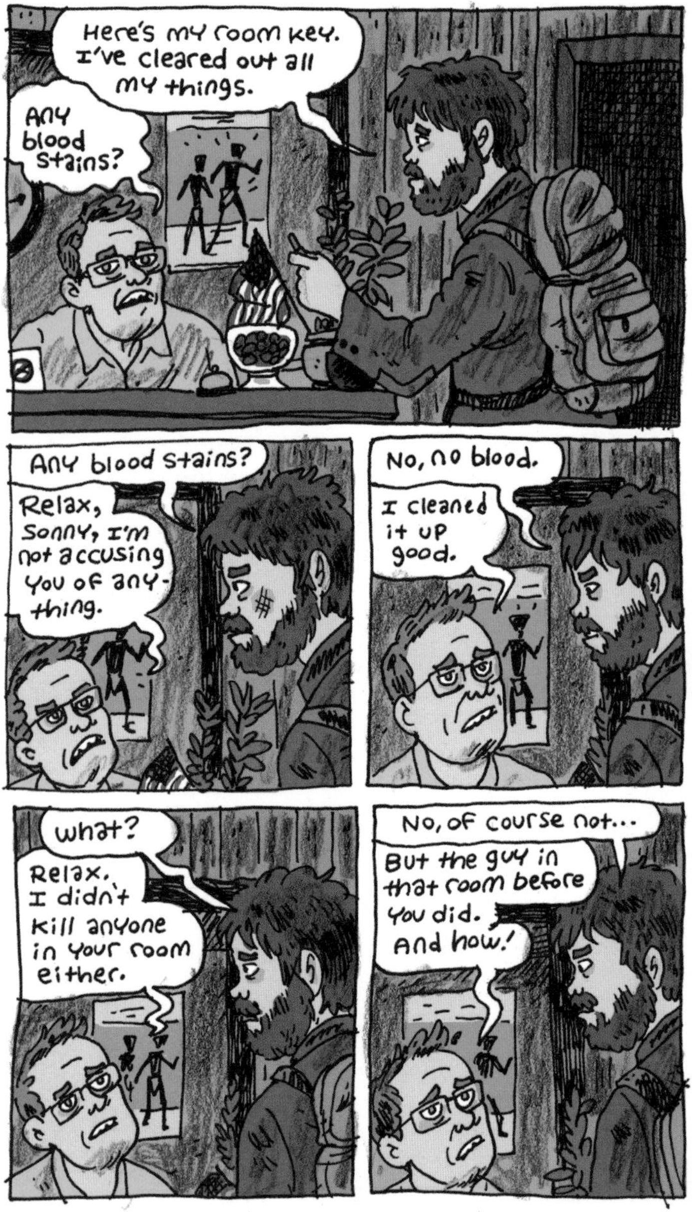
Here's my room key. I've cleared out all my things.
Any blood stains?
Any blood stains?
Relax, sonny, I'm not accusing you of anything.
No, no blood.
I cleaned it up good.
what?
Relax. I didn't kill anyone in your room either.
No, of course not...
But the guy in that room before you did. And how!

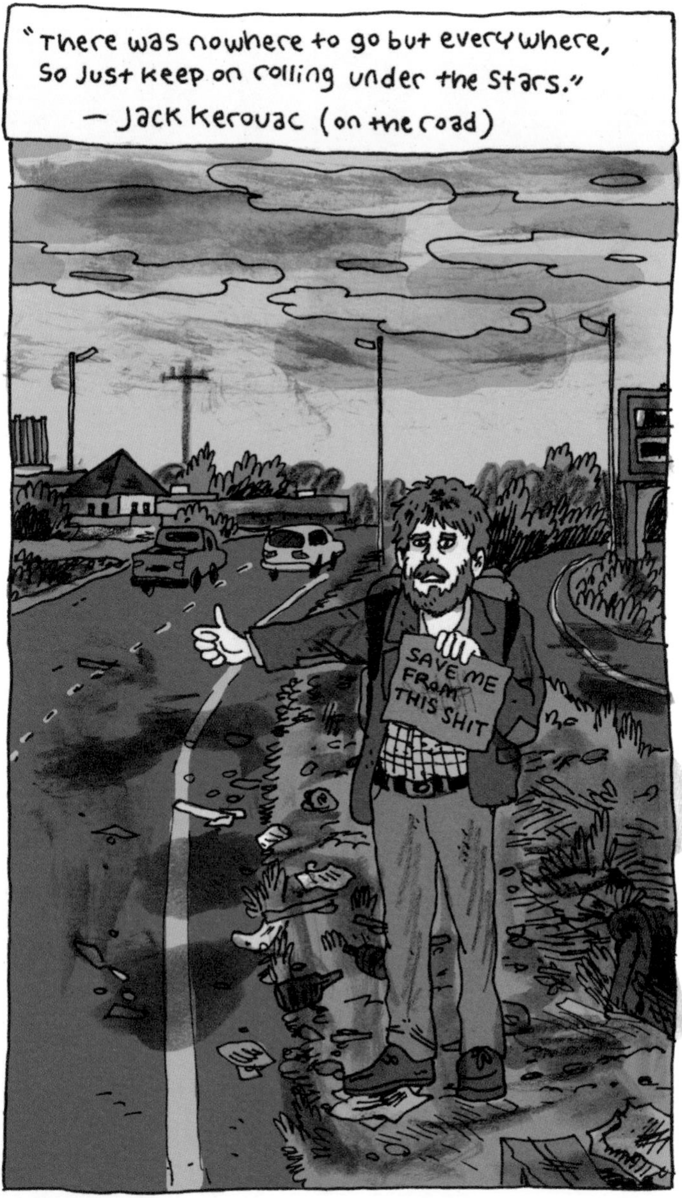
"There was nowhere to go but everywhere, so just keep on rolling under the stars."
— Jack Kerouac (on the road)
SAVE ME FROM THIS SHIT

FANTE HAS NO CAR

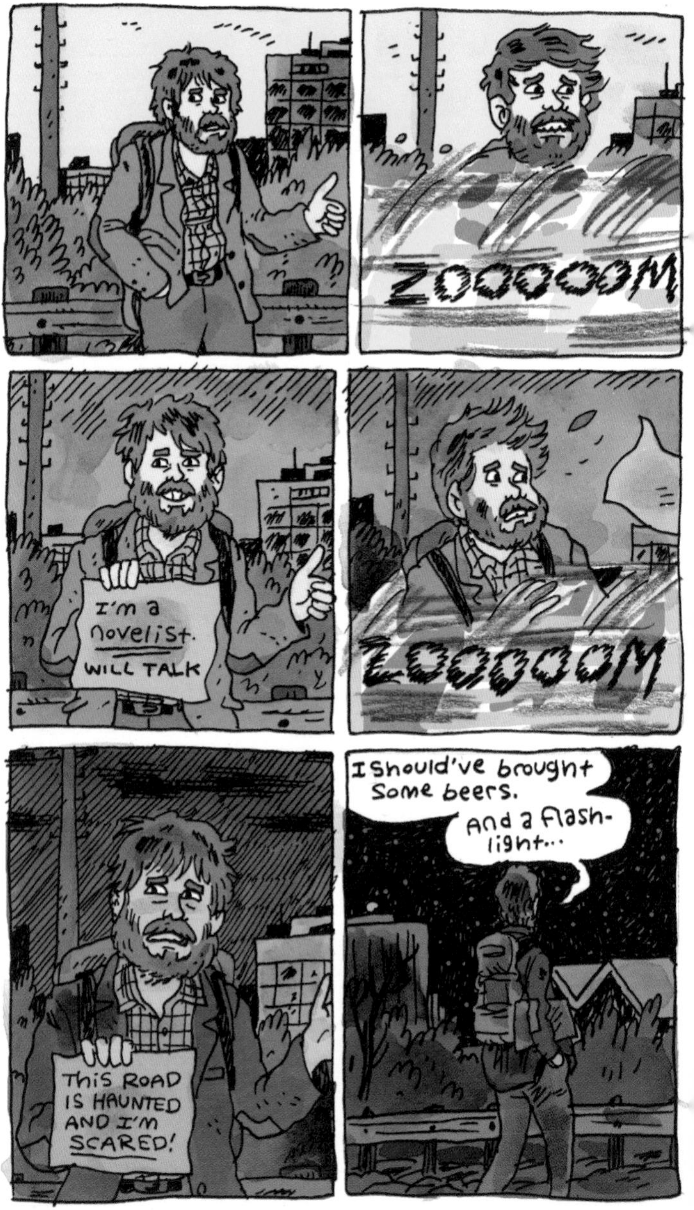

ZOOOOOM
I'm a novelist.
WILL TALK
ZOOOOOOM
THIS ROAD IS HAUNTED AND I'M SCARED!
I should've brought some beers.
And a flash-light...

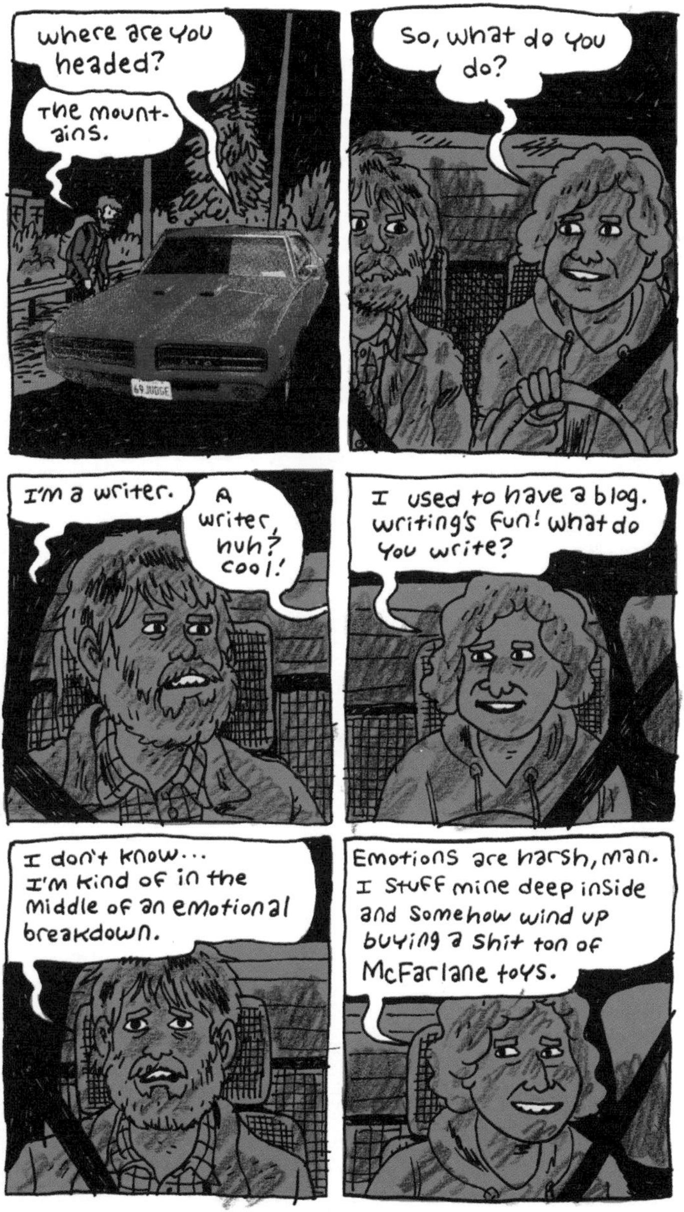
Where are you headed?
The mount-ains.
69 JUDGE
So, what do you do?
I'm a writer.
A writer, huh? cool!
I used to have a blog. writing's fun! what do you write?
I don't know... I'm kind of in the middle of an emotional breakdown.
Emotions are harsh, man. I stuff mine deep inside and somehow wind up buying a shit ton of McFarlane toys.

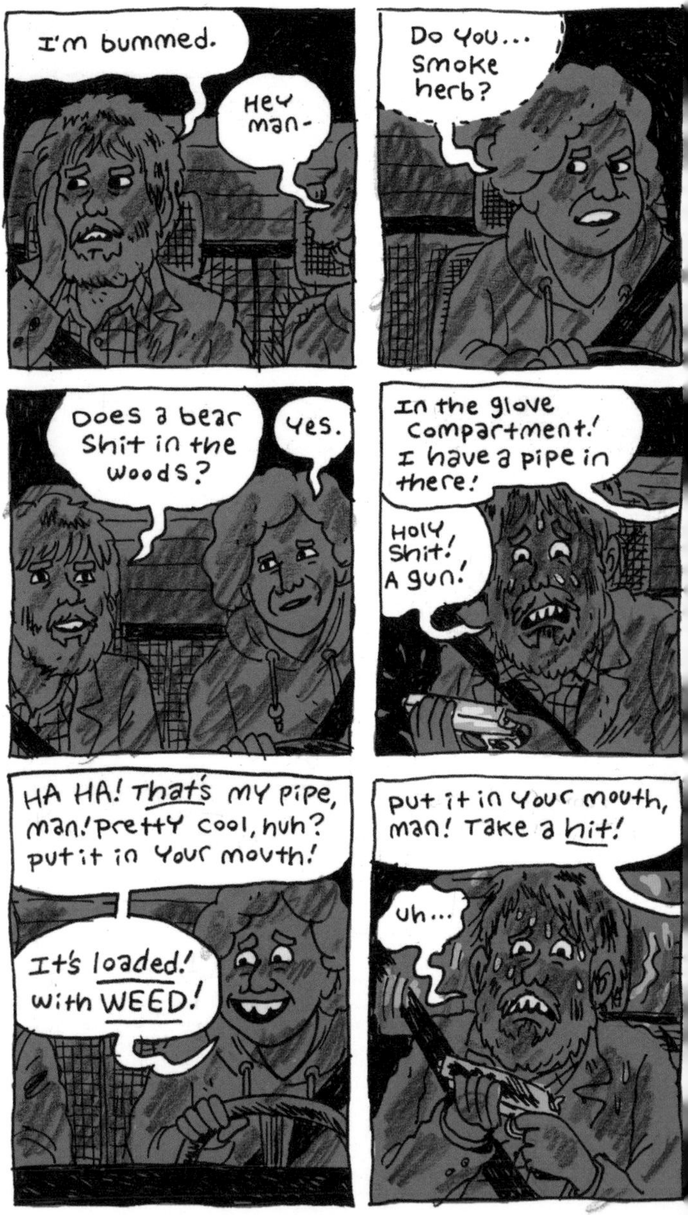
I'm bummed.
Hey man-
Do you... smoke herb?
Does a bear shit in the woods?
Yes.
In the glove compartment! I have a pipe in there!
Holy shit! A gun!
HA HA! That's my pipe, man! pretty cool, huh? put it in your mouth!
It's loaded! with WEED!
put it in your mouth, man! Take a hit!
uh...

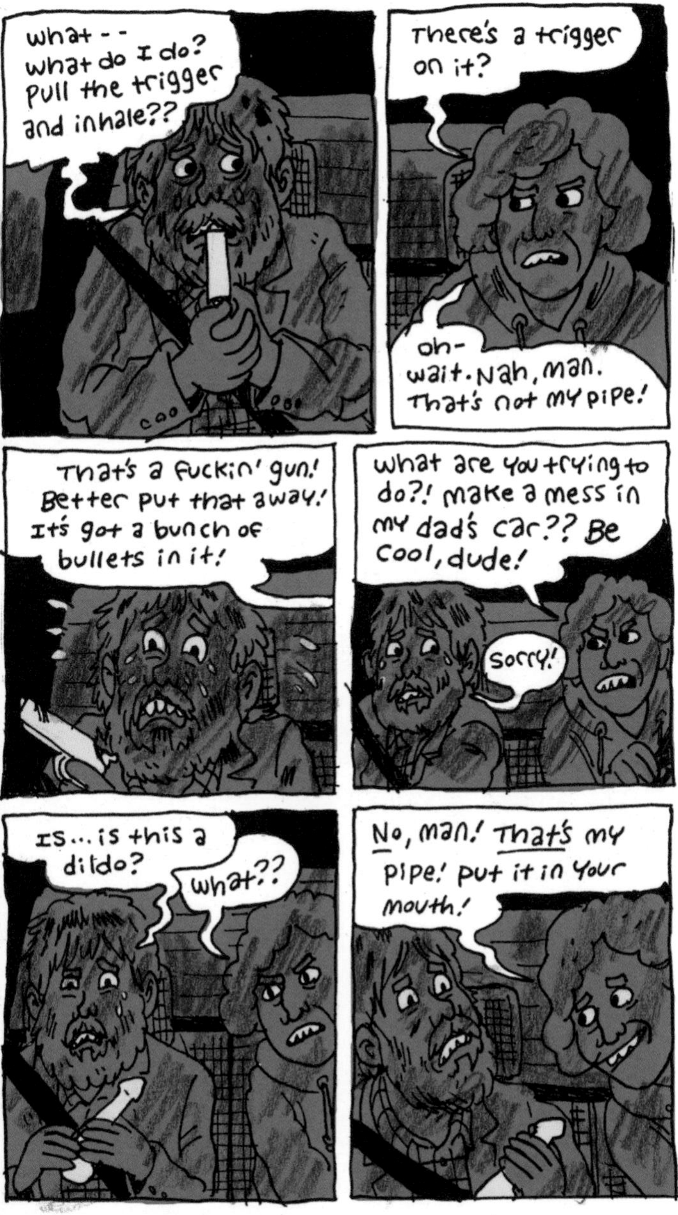
what--
what do I do?
pull the trigger
and inhale??
There's a trigger
on it?
oh-
wait. Nah, man.
That's not my pipe!
That's a fuckin' gun!
Better put that away!
It's got a bunch of
bullets in it!
What are you trying to
do?! Make a mess in
my dad's car?? Be
cool, dude!
Sorry!
Is... is this a
dildo?
what??
No, man! That's my
pipe! put it in your
mouth!

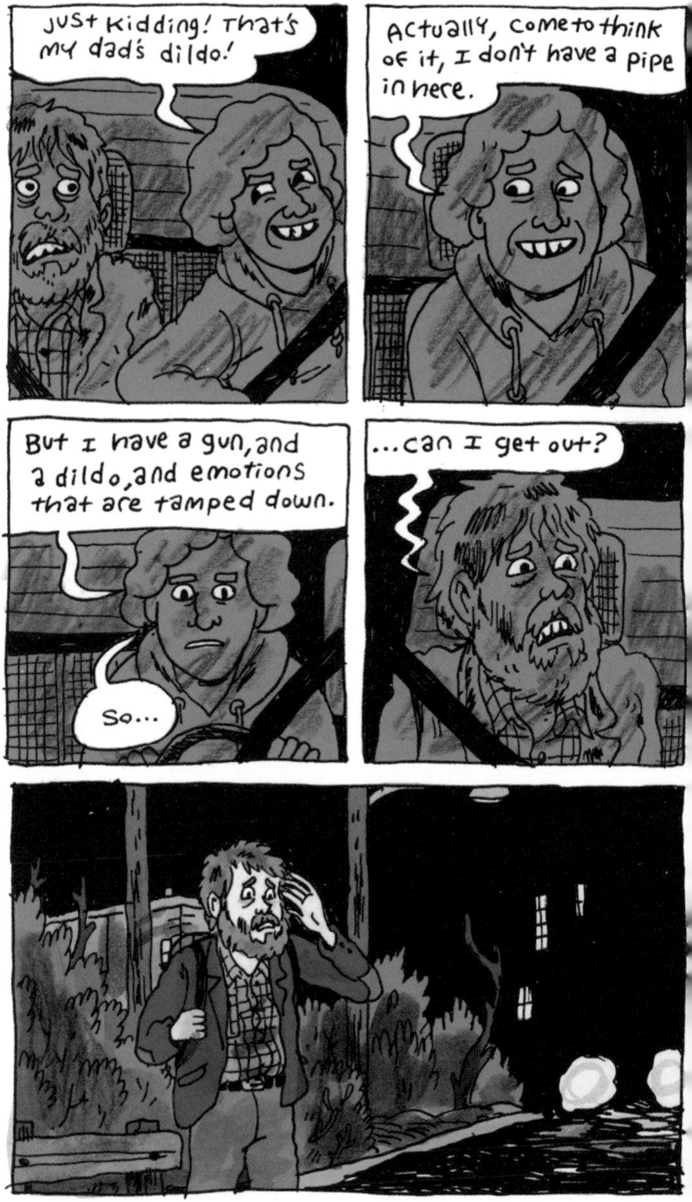
Just Kidding! That's my dad's dildo!
Actually, come to think of it, I don't have a pipe in here.
But I have a gun, and a dildo, and emotions that are tamped down.
So...
...can I get out?

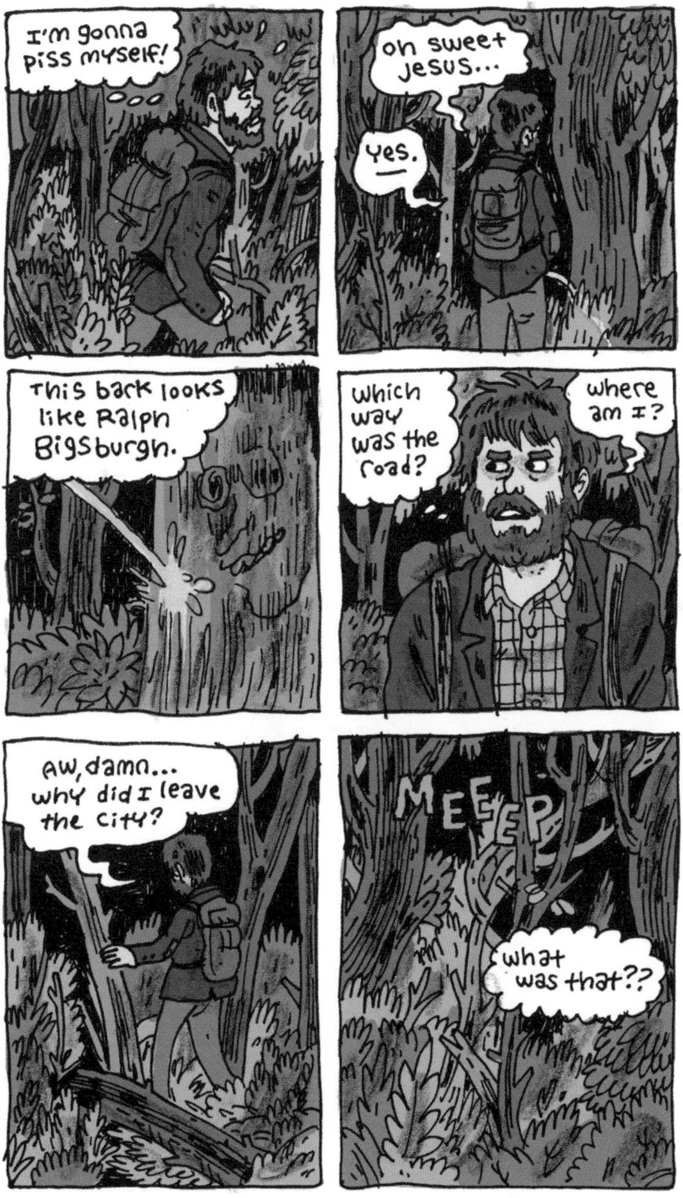
I'm gonna piss myself!
oh sweet jesus...
yes.
This bark looks like Ralph Bigsburgh.
which way was the road?
where am I?
aw, damn... why did I leave the city?
MEEEP
what was that??

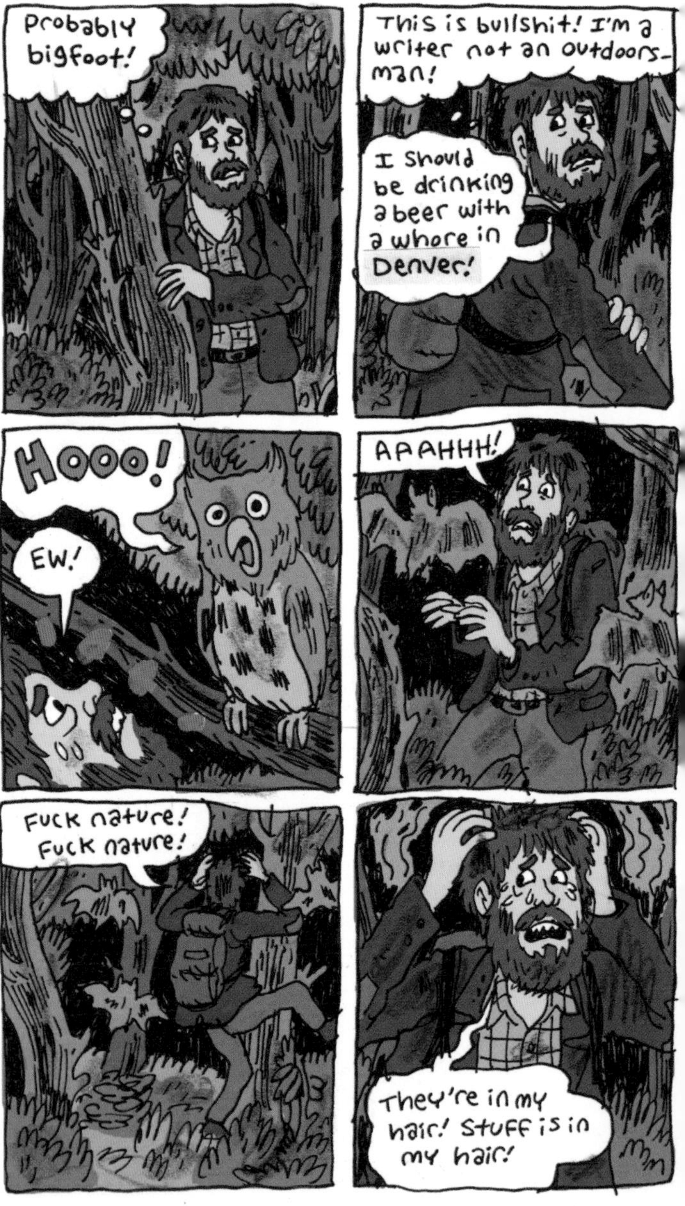
Probably bigfoot!
This is bullshit! I'm a writer not an outdoorsman!
I should be drinking a beer with a whore in Denver!
HOOO!
EW!
AAAHHH!
Fuck nature! Fuck nature!
They're in my hair! Stuff is in my hair!

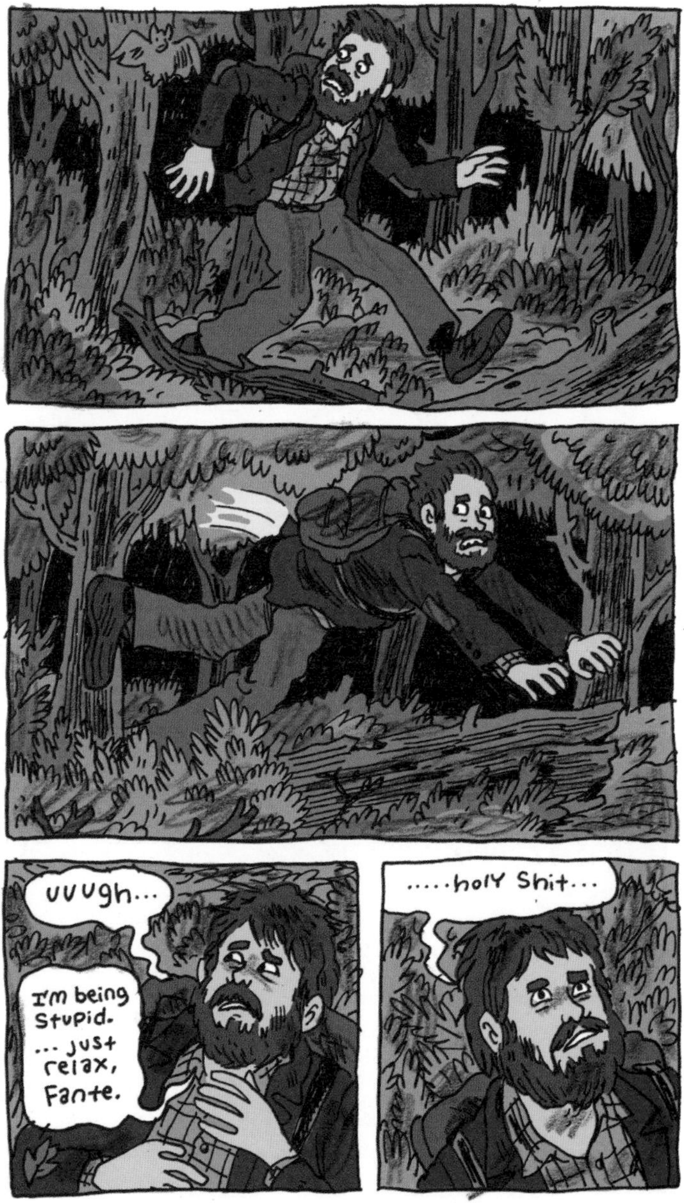
uuugh...
I'm being stupid. ... just relax, Fante.
.....holy Shit...

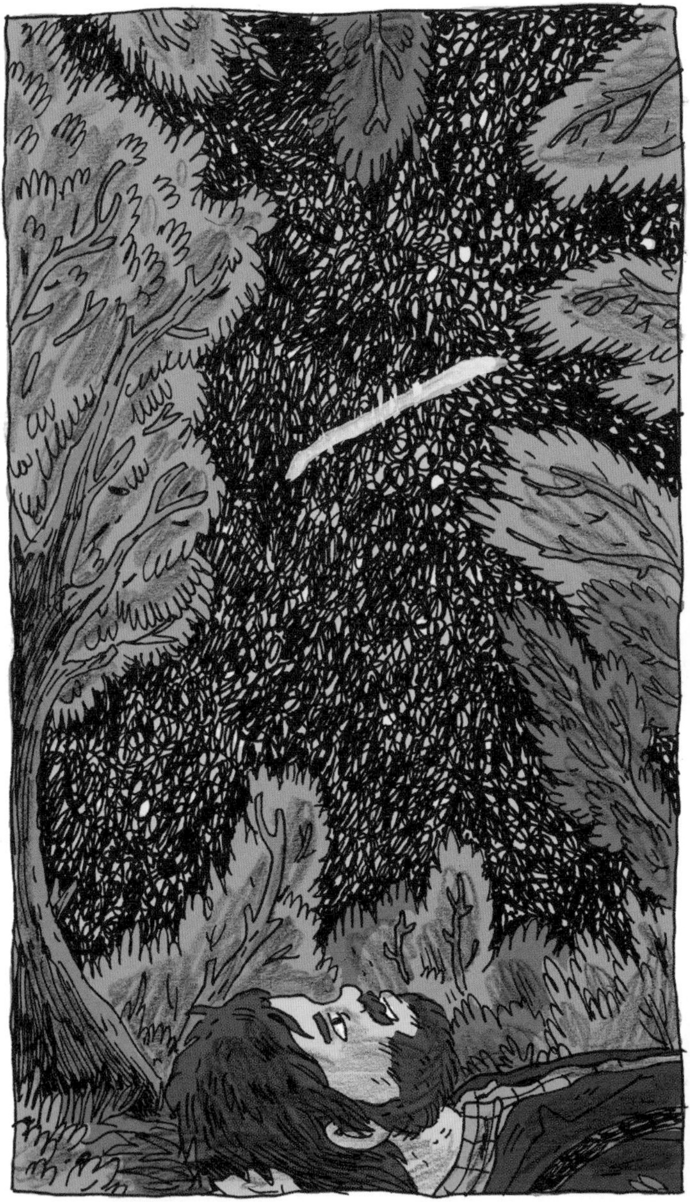

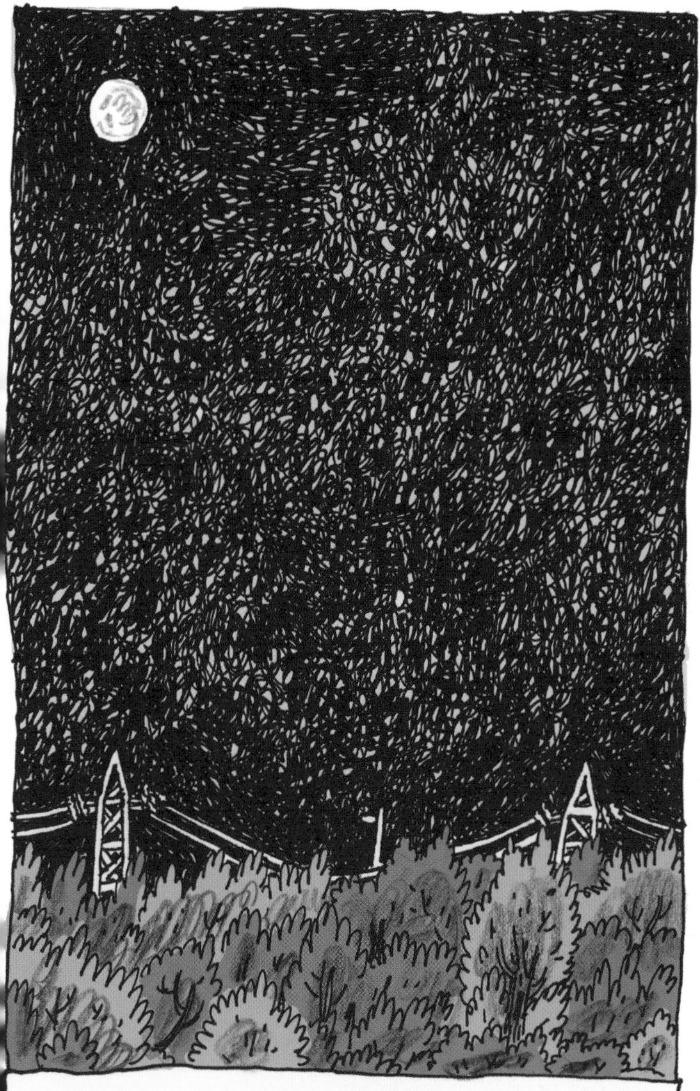

"There is no real ending. It's just the place where you stop the story."

~ Frank Herbert

THE
END

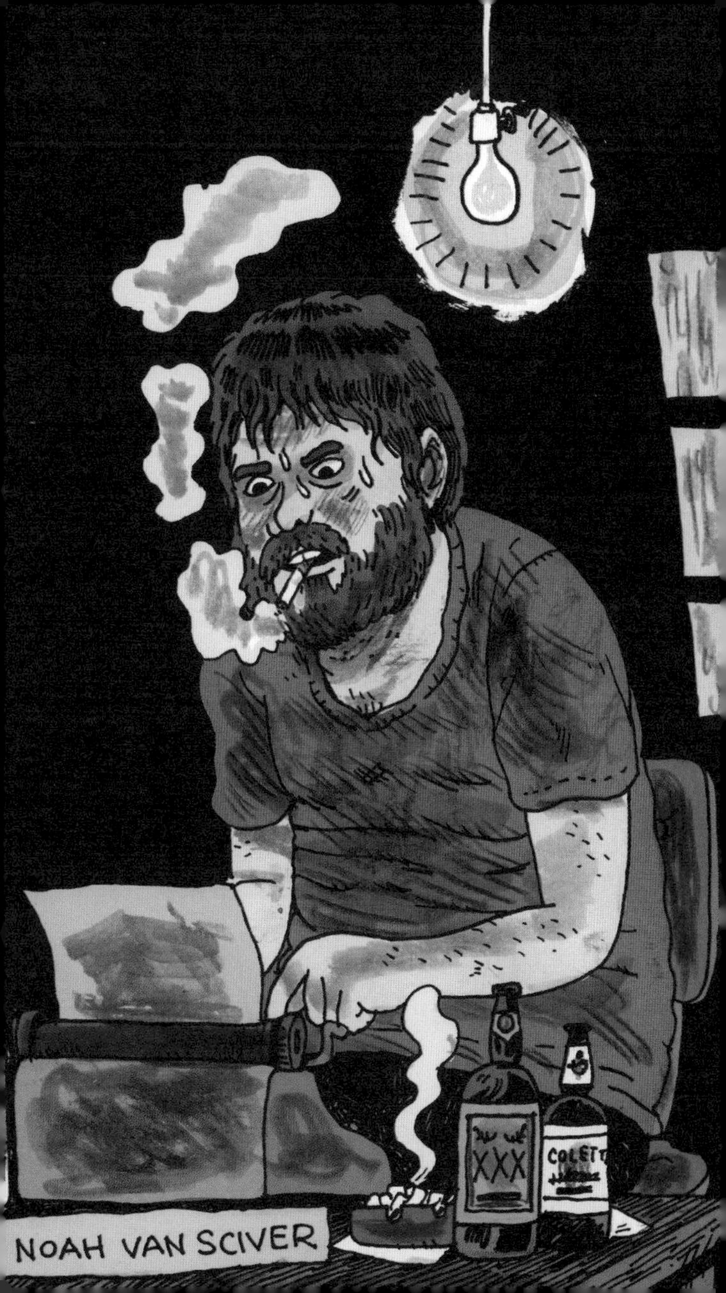
NOAH VAN SCIVER
XXX

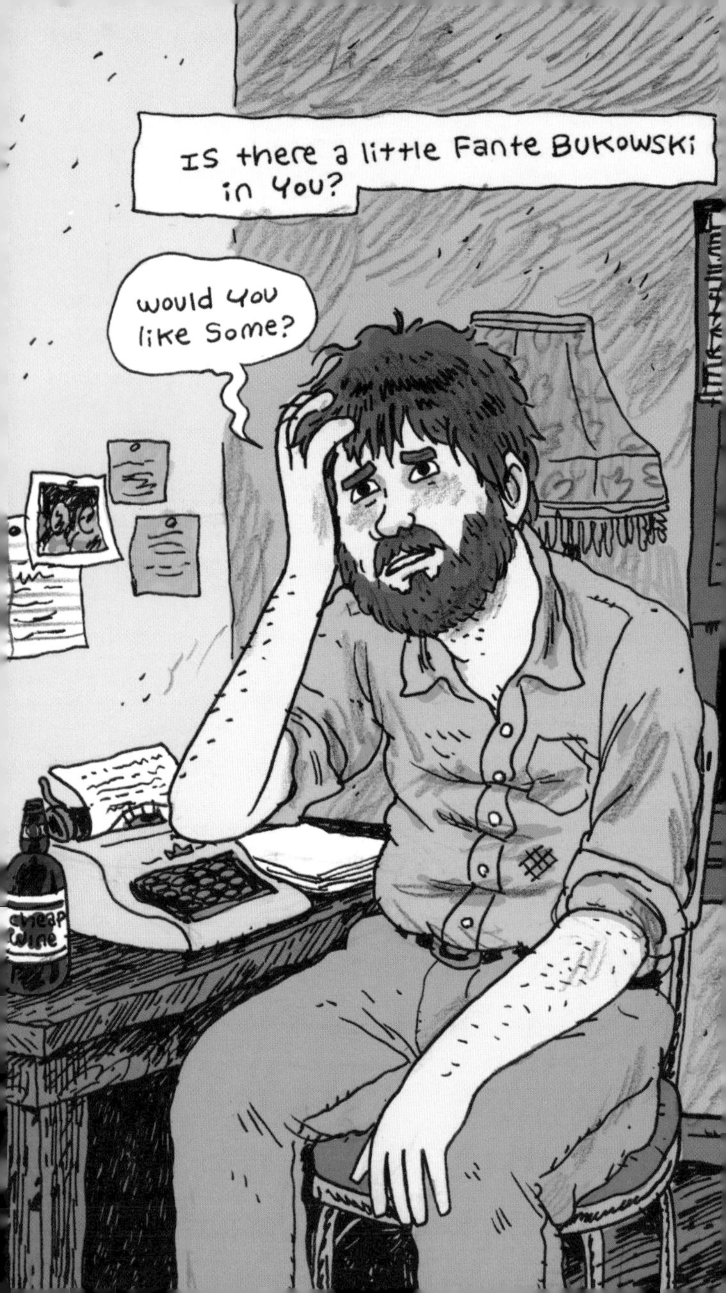
Is there a little Fante Bukowski in You?
would You like Some?
cheap wine

FANTE BUKOWSKI
PIN-UPS:
ZAK SALLY
JOHN PORCELLINO
JESSE JACOBS
JOSEPH REMNANT
LESLIE STEIN
ERIC REYNOLDS

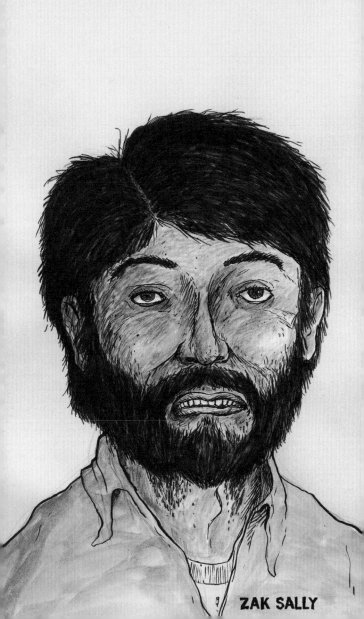

ZAK SALLY

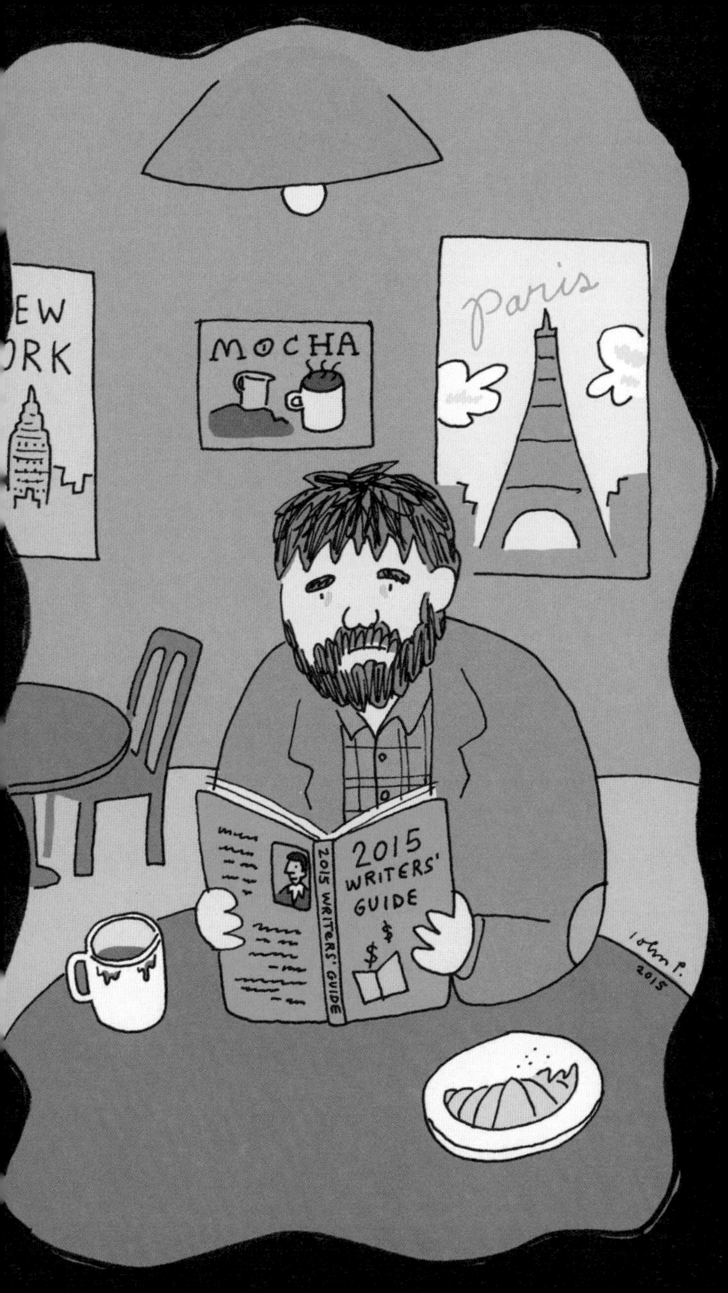

MOCHA
Paris
2015 WRITERS' GUIDE
2015 WRITERS' GUIDE
$
$
John P.
2015

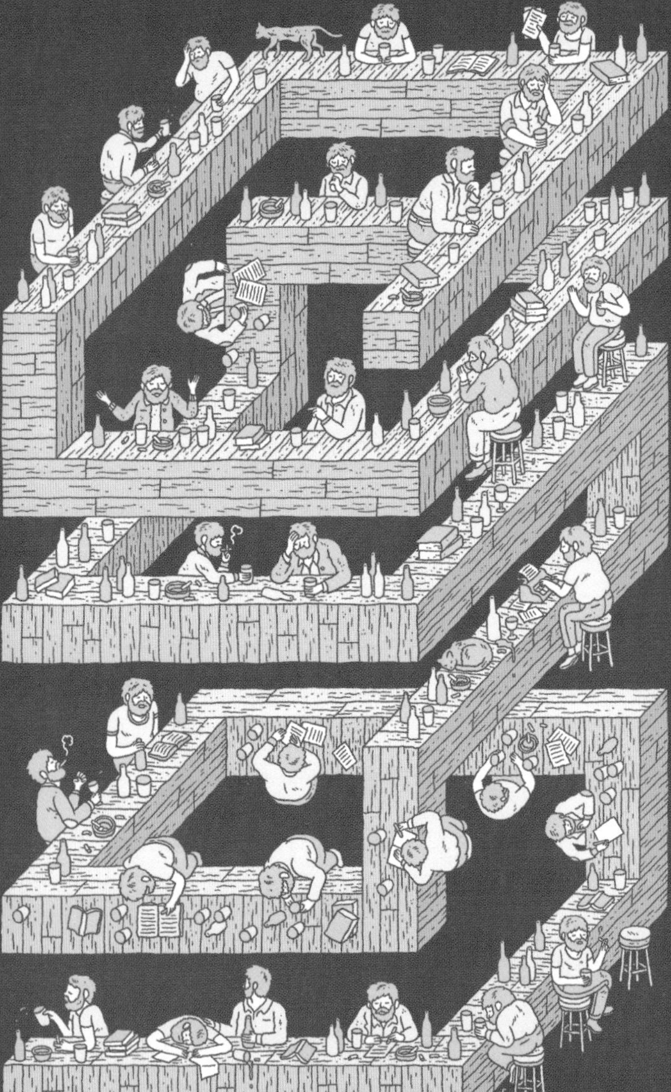
JJACOBS

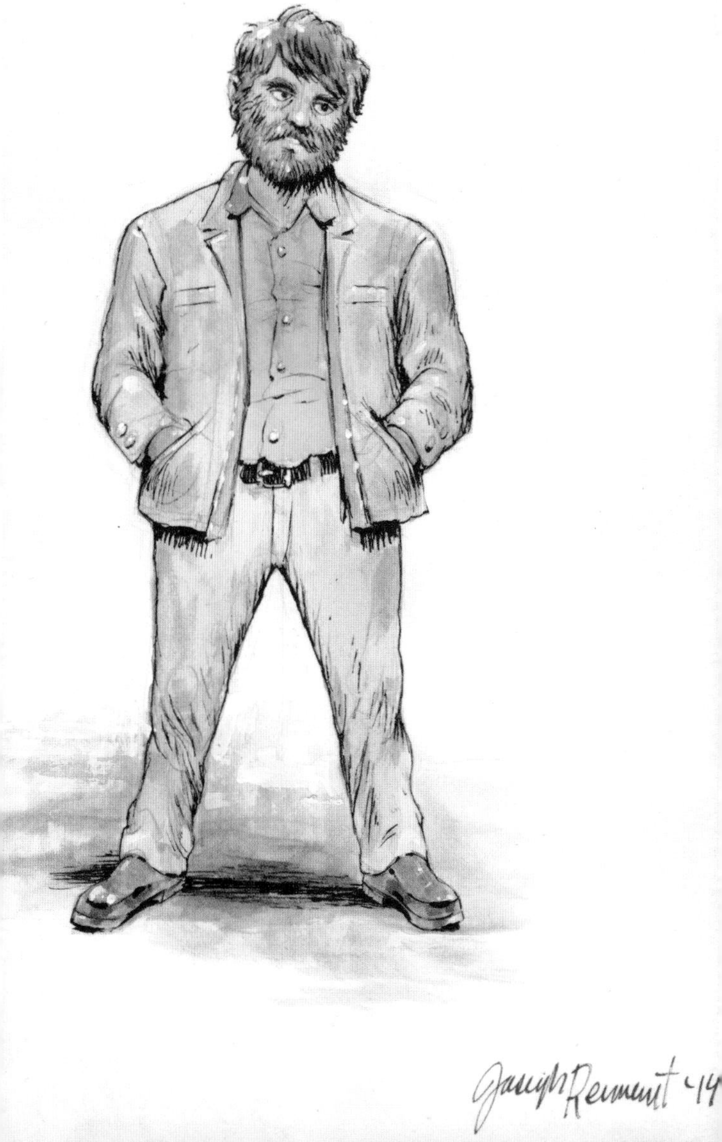

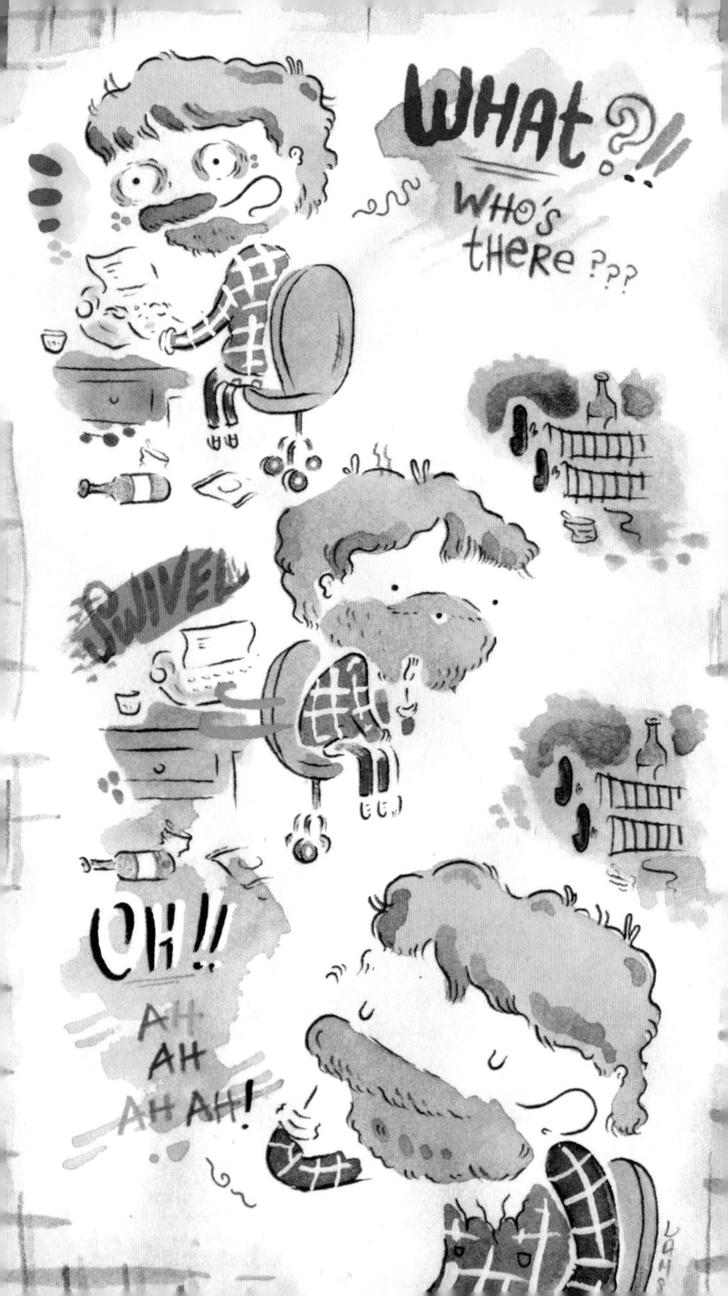
WHAT?!!
WHO'S THERE???
SWIVEL
OH!!
AH AH AH AH!
LAMS

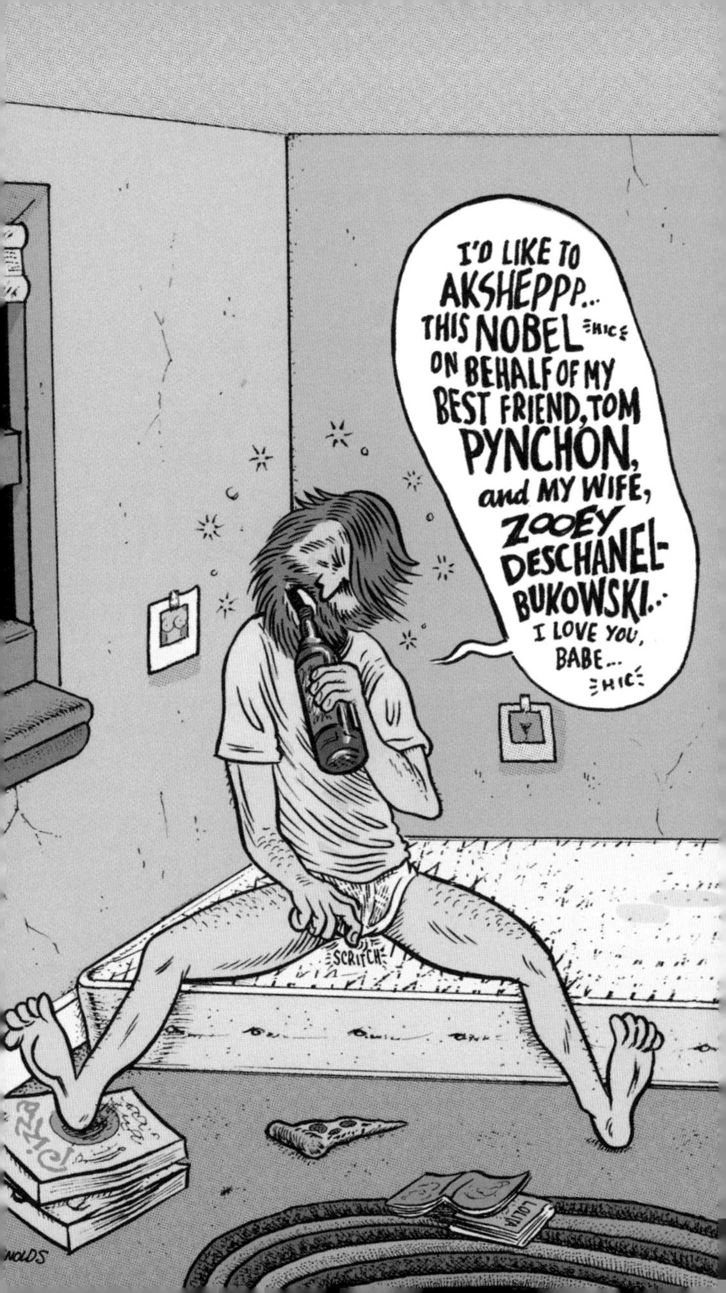
I'D LIKE TO AKSHEPPP... THIS NOBEL =HIC= ON BEHALF OF MY BEST FRIEND, TOM PYNCHON, and MY WIFE, ZOOEY DESCHANEL-BUKOWSKI... I LOVE YOU, BABE... =HIC=
SCRITCH

Noah van Sciver is a
well-known and admired
cartoonist. And he's
wealthy.
noahvansciver.tumblr.com